Hit The Drums!

Fast & Easy Beginner Method

ISBN 978-90-9034274-0

AF471831

Hit The Drums!
Marco Mepschen
Drumset

www.hitthedrums.com

Photography: Dirk Hoogendoorn - Moens
Adaptation: Marco Mepschen

Published in-house

INHOUD

ABOUT MARCO MEPSCHEN

Marco Mepschen (1983) already knew from a young age that he wanted to become a drummer, which is why he started drumming in music school at age 8. After a year he also played in drum bands and orchestras.

When he was 15 years old, he started playing in different bands. Shortly after that he started the preliminary training of the conservatory. After this preliminary training he was accepted into the conservatory of Zwolle.

Since 2000 he has been touring through the Netherlands with his band and has performed in numerous concerts in cafes, clubs, theatres and on festivals in the past 20 years. He has also recorded multiple singles and albums.

In 2012 he established his own drum school. As a drum teacher he teaches a wide array of students on a daily basis, with pupils ranging from young to old, and from beginners to advanced.

It's his passion to pass on his extensive knowledge and experience and he loves seeing his students getting excited about drumming and music!

HOW TO USE THIS BOOK

This book covers the two most important facets a drummer needs to master: grooves and fills.
In the chapter that will focus on grooves, you will learn how to play new grooves through coordination exercises. In the chapters that will focus on fills, you will learn a different rhythmical figure every time.
We will combine these different rhythmical figures to make new fills.

Every chapter in this book covers material that builds on the previous chapters. As you are going through the book, you will notice that it takes you less and less effort to master new fills and grooves.

LEARNING TO READ MUSICAL NOTATION

Learning to read notes gives you a lot of advantages. It may seem tricky at first, but musical notation is easy and basically simple math. The notation contains figures you will learn to recognize in time. It is the same as learning words, which you can then use to form sentences and read. By learning musical notation, you will be able to consult countless sources besides this book, like the internet and other books, to further develop yourself.

Most songs and grooves are in a 4/4-time signature. That means that there are four quarter notes in each bar. We can then further divide the quarter notes in eighths and sixteenths. We count quarter notes as "one-two-three-four". The eighths we count as 1-& 2-& 3-& 4-&.
The sixteenths we count as 1-e-&-a 2-e-&-a 3-e-&-a 4-e-&-a (pronounce it as "e-and-ah").
Try to pronounce the rhythm like this first, before you actually start to play.
This way you will get an idea of how the rhythm will sound and you will notice that this will make the actual playing of the rhythm easier. If you also pronounce it out loud whilst drumming, it will help you to learn to play the groove or fill better.

HOW TO USE THIS BOOK

NOTATIE

Every part of the drum set has its own note symbol and place on the staff.

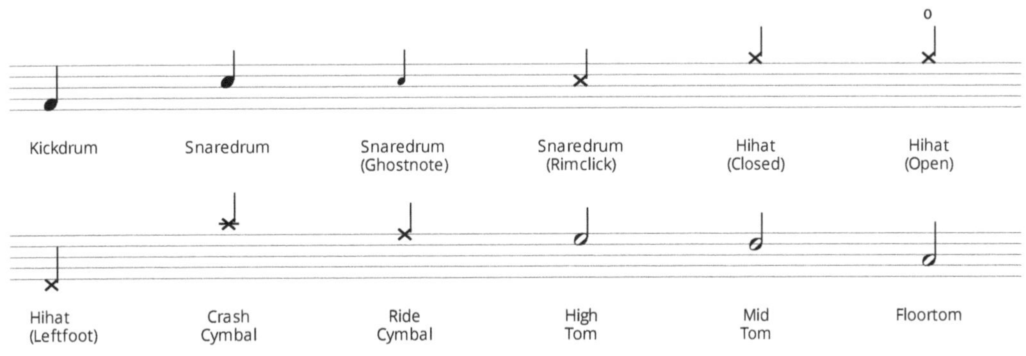

In this book we use the following repeat signs:

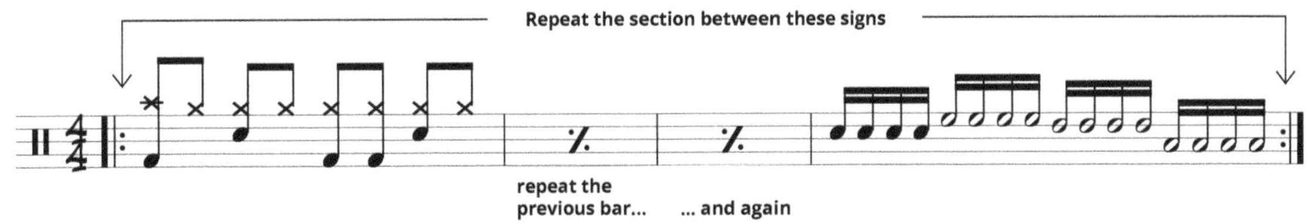

HOW TO USE THIS BOOK

STICKING

In many exercises the sticking is mentioned together with the notes.
This way you will know which hand or foot needs to play the note. R = right hand, L = left hand, K = right foot (kick drum) and LF = left foot (hi-hat pedal).

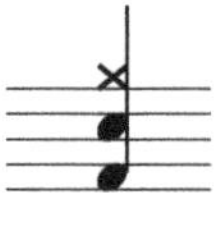

R+L+K

Sometimes multiple notes are written above one another. This means that you need to play different parts of the drum set at the same time. In the case of the image, you play the upper note with the right hand, the middle note with the left hand and the lower note with the right foot.

In this book we assume to have a right-handed drummer. If you are left-handed, it becomes R = left hand, L = right hand and if you are also left legged it becomes B = left foot (hi-hat pedal) and LF = right foot (kick drum).

COORDINATION EXCERCISES

Coordination exercises are written in a grey box. These are exercises that will help with being able to play a difficult part of a complete groove. We are basically putting a part of the groove under a magnifying glass. By splitting up and repeating the difficult parts of a groove or fill, you will be able to eventually play any complicated groove or fill. Start by playing the exercise in a slow tempo. Keep increasing the tempo while you repeat the exercise.

TEMPO

Tempo

55 75 110

Three tempos in BPM (beats per minute) will usually be mentioned at the top of the chapter. You could use a metronome or click track with these tempos. You can download free click tracks at www.thuisdrummen.nl. The purpose is to play the exercises in all three tempos. You first play all the exercises in the slowest tempo mentioned. If this succeeds, you then play all the exercises in the next tempo.

FOCUS ON FEELING

During practice it can happen that you are focused too much on reading the notes, because of which you can't feel the groove or fill very well. You could try playing the exercise from memory so you can focus on the feeling. This way you will focus more on your body's movements and what the exercise sounds like. You will remember the groove or fill better as well and will be able to play it at a later time without thinking during a song.

HOW TO USE THIS BOOK

GROOVES PRACTICE TIPS

You practically always play the grooves from this book with the right hand on the hi-hat. Also try to play a different part of the drum set with your right hand, like the ride cymbal, floor tom, snare drum or on the side of the drum.

To check whether you master a groove well, you need to play the groove in a scheme.
Such a scheme can look as followed:

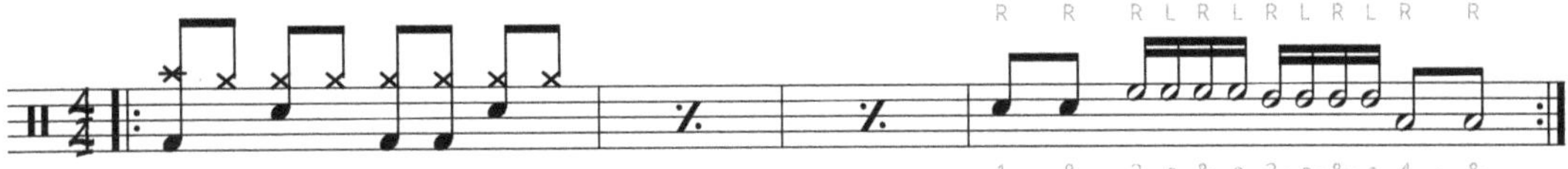

You start the scheme with a crash cymbal on the first beat of the groove, after which you continue the groove on the hi-hat. You play the groove three times, then a random fill follows. Repeat this scheme a couple of times.

Make sure you keep the tempo constant and keep playing the right groove after the transition from fill to groove. Also try to play an entire scheme with your right hand on a different part of the drum set.

FILLS PRACTICE TIPS

In the chapters that cover fills you will every time learn one rhythmical figure. In the section "grooves with fills" you will combine this new figure with the previously learned rhythmical figures to make fills. Also try to create fills yourself by combining the rhythmical figures.

You can also divide the different notes of a rhythmical figure over different parts of the drum set.
As an example, you can play the first note of the figure on the snare drum and the other notes on the toms. This makes it possible to create an unending number of fills!

During the fill you can also play the kick drum (A) or the hi-hat with the left foot (B) on every beat.

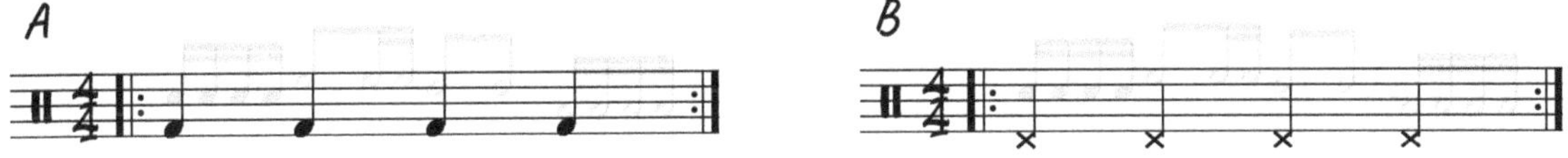

HITTHEDRUMS.COM

All of the exercises from this book are explained and played in videos on the website www.hitthedrums.com. You will also find a wide array of additional exercises, useful downloads and a list of songs that contain the grooves from this book. This way you will be able to start playing your favorite song right away!

1 - INTRODUCTION - *Basic quarter note groove*

You play one stroke on the ride cymbal on every beat. This note is called the quarter note. We play four beats (four quarter notes) in one bar. Start slow and count out loud. Make sure the tempo stays constant and try not to speed up or slow down. Repeat every exercise at least eight times. Do the same thing again, but this time in a faster tempo. Repetition is important to train your body in independent movement coordination.

Exercises for basic quarter note groove

A
R R R R
1 2 3 4

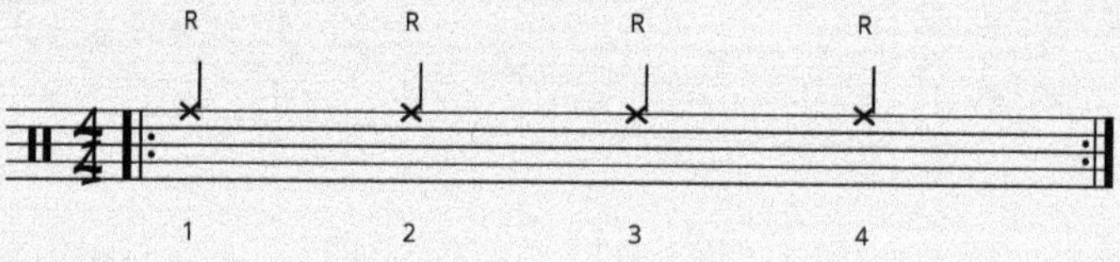

B
R+L R+L R+L R+L
1 2 3 4

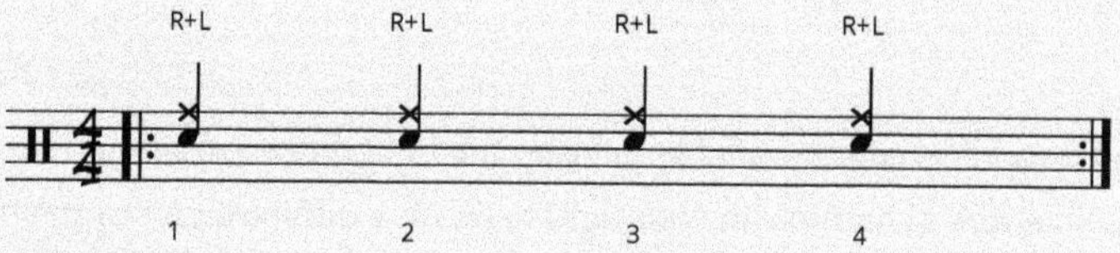

C
R+K R+K R+K R+K
1 2 3 4

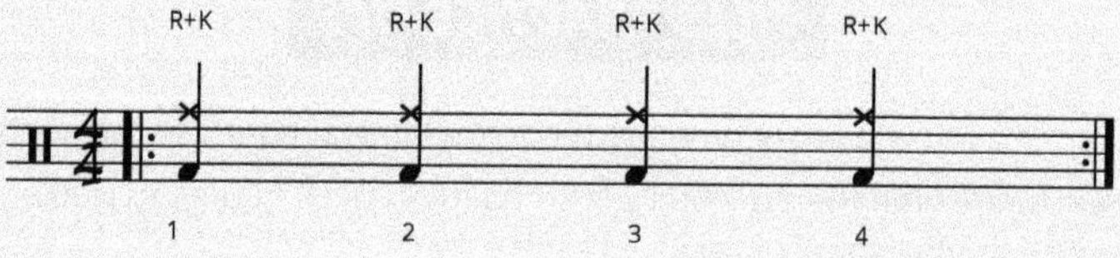

D
R+L R+L R+L R+L R+K R+K R+K R+K
1 2 3 4 1 2 3 4

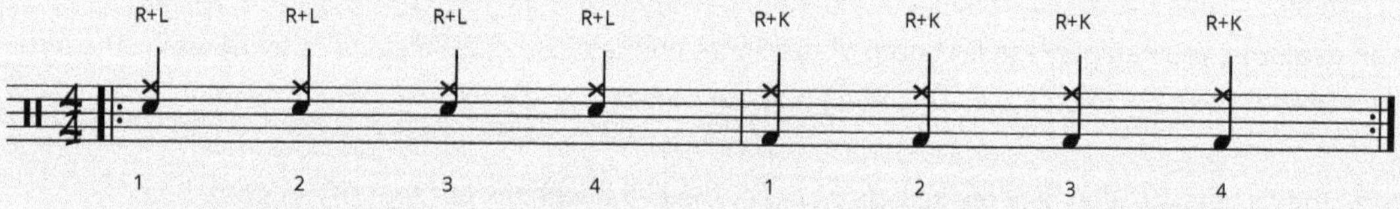

E
R+K R+K R+L R+L
1 2 3 4

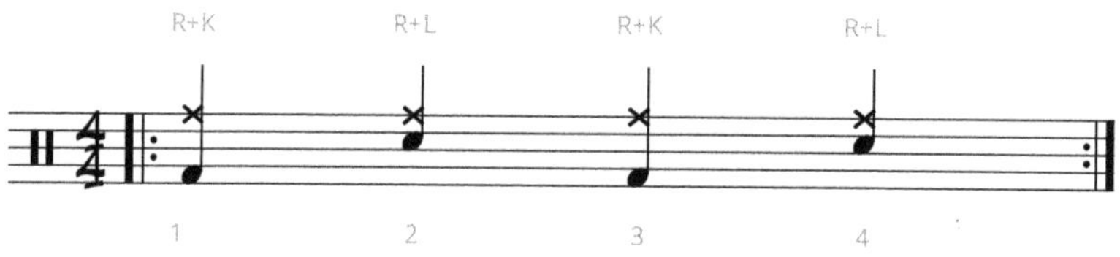

R+K R+L R+K R+L
1 2 3 4

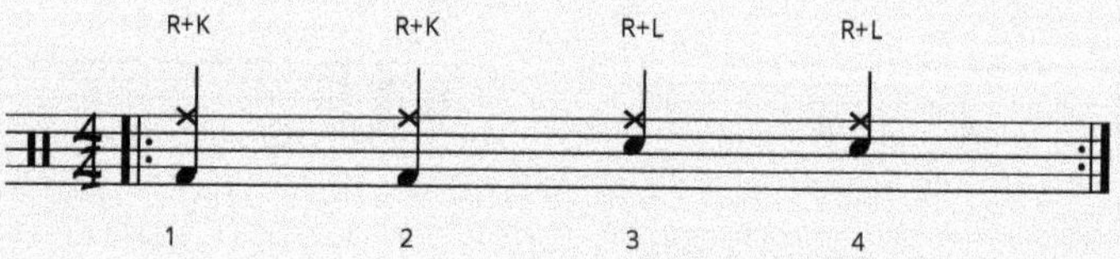

Play the exercises once more, but now with the right hand on the hi-hat.
The right arm crosses the left arm here over the top.

2 - INTRODUCTION - *Basic eighth note groove*

With the basic quarter note groove you played one hi-hat stroke per beat. Now you are going to divide the beat in two strokes: one stroke on the beat and another stroke exactly in between the beats. You can make it easier on yourself by saying "and" in between the beats: 1-& 2-& 3-& 4-&. There are now eight strokes in a bar (eight eighth notes). Start slow and count out loud. Make sure the tempo stays constant and try not to speed up or slow down. Repeat every exercise at least eight times. Do the same thing again, but this time in a faster tempo.

Exercises for basic eighth note groove

A

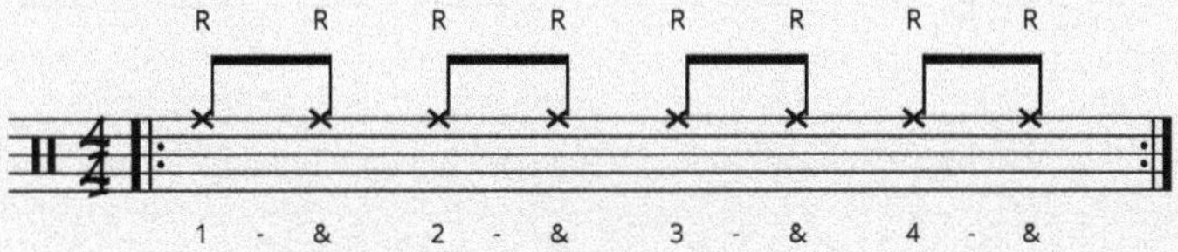

R R R R R R R R

1 - & 2 - & 3 - & 4 - &

B

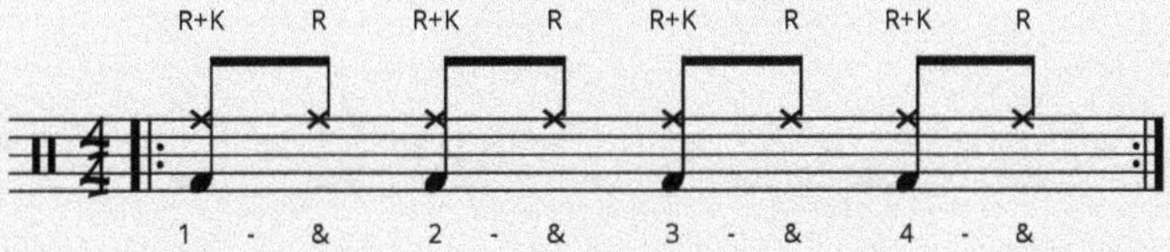

R+K R R+K R R+K R R+K R

1 - & 2 - & 3 - & 4 - &

C

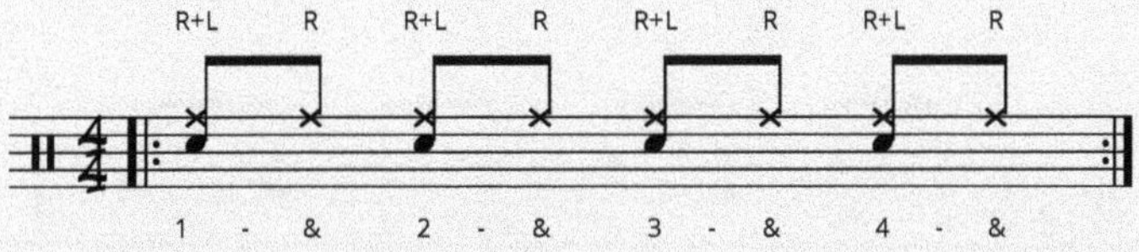

R+L R R+L R R+L R R+L R

1 - & 2 - & 3 - & 4 - &

D

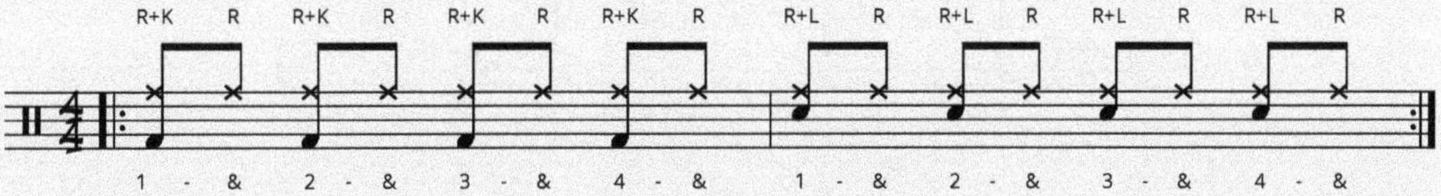

R+K R R+K R R+K R R+K R R+L R R+L R R+L R R+L R

1 - & 2 - & 3 - & 4 - & 1 - & 2 - & 3 - & 4 - &

E

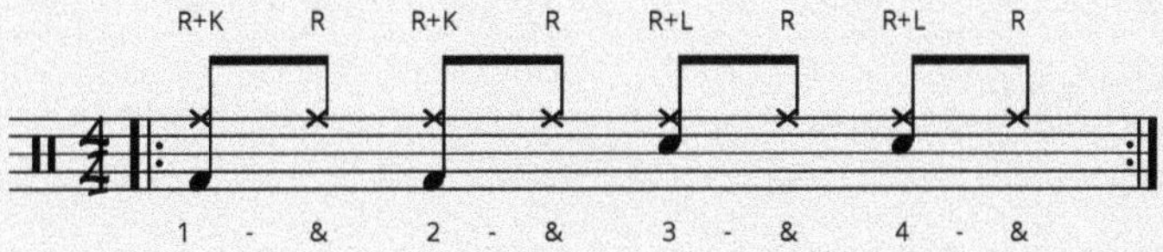

R+K R R+K R R+L R R+L R

1 - & 2 - & 3 - & 4 - &

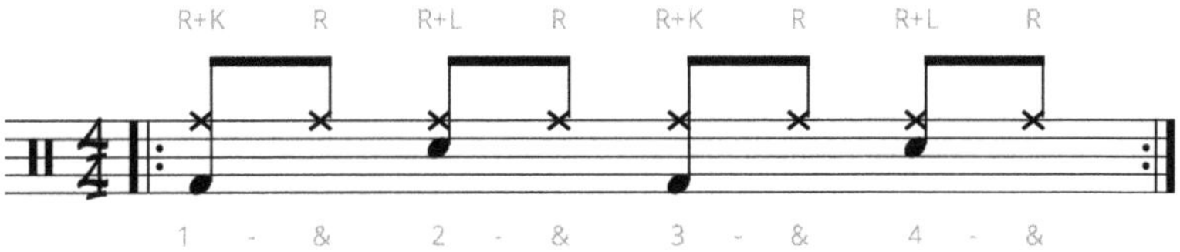

R+K R R+L R R+K R R+L R

1 - & 2 - & 3 - & 4 - &

Play the exercises once more, but now with the right hand on the hi-hat.
The right arm crosses the left arm here over the top.

3 - GROOVES - *Eighth note hi-hat #1*

With a groove we mean a repetitive series of rhythmical figures that we play on the hi-hat or ride, together with the snare drum and kick drum. Another word for groove is rhythm or beat.
With grooves in eighths we play eighth notes on the hi-hat. The snare drum is played mostly on the second and fourth beat (the back beats). Groove 1 is the basic eighth note groove. Groove 2 until 10 are all kick drum variations of groove 1.

Tempo

30 60 100

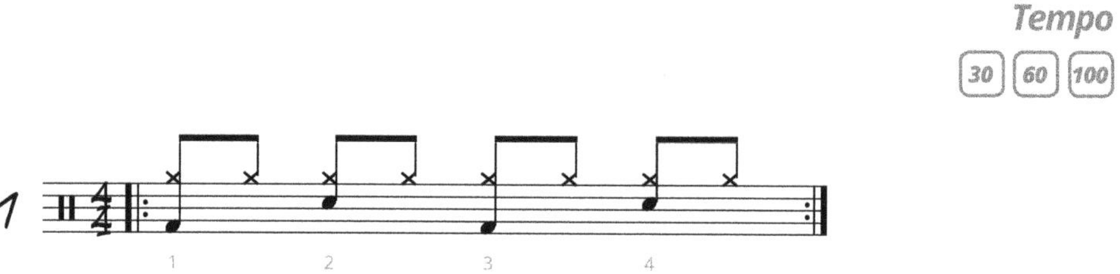

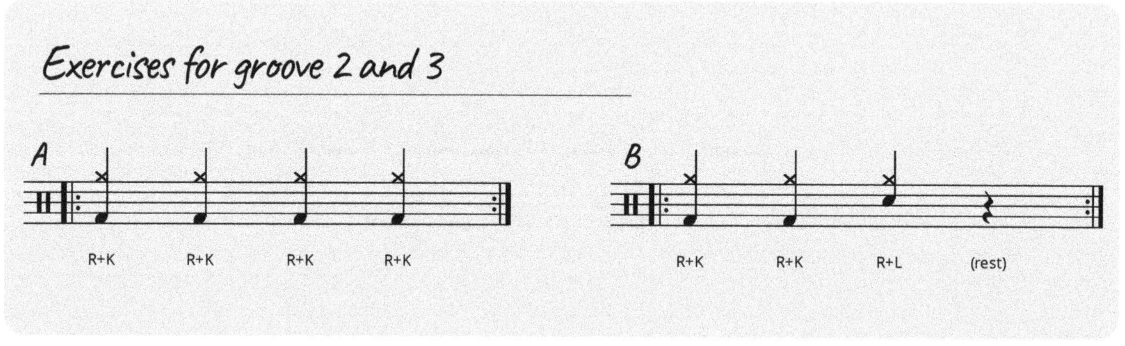

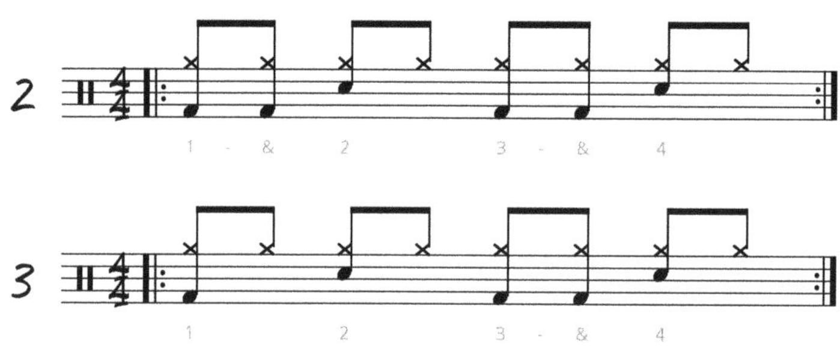

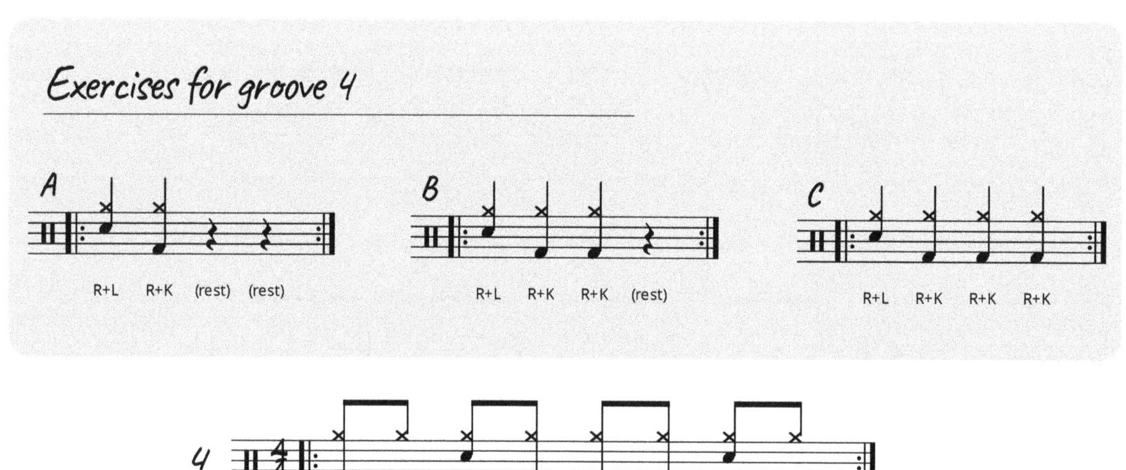

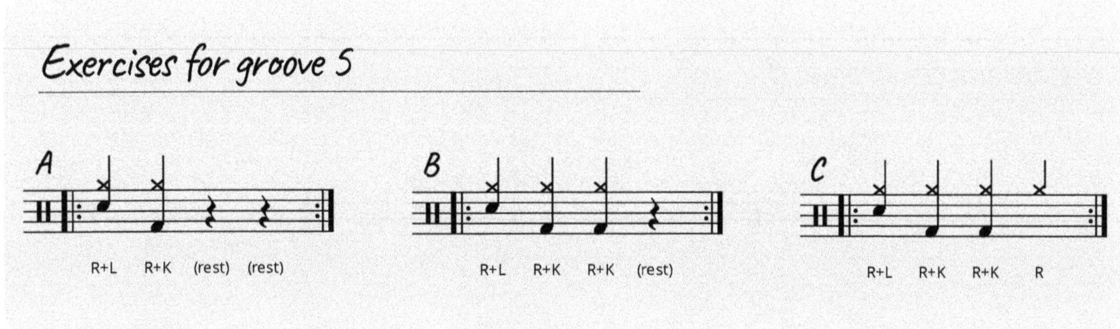
Exercises for groove 5
A
R+L R+K (rest) (rest)
B
R+L R+K R+K (rest)
C
R+L R+K R+K R

5
1 2 - & 3 4

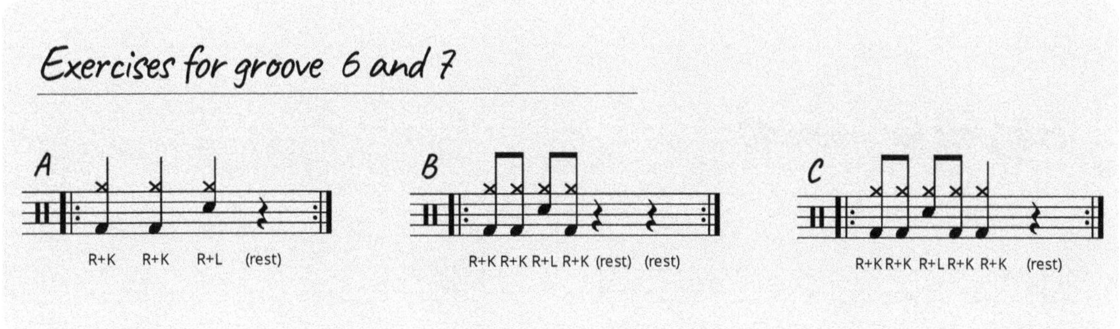
Exercises for groove 6 and 7
A
R+K R+K R+L (rest)
B
R+K R+K R+L R+K (rest) (rest)
C
R+K R+K R+L R+K R+K (rest)

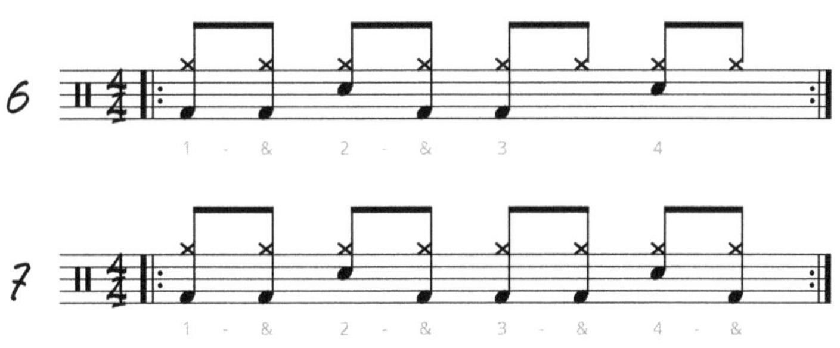
6
1 - & 2 - & 3 4
7
1 - & 2 - & 3 - & 4 - &

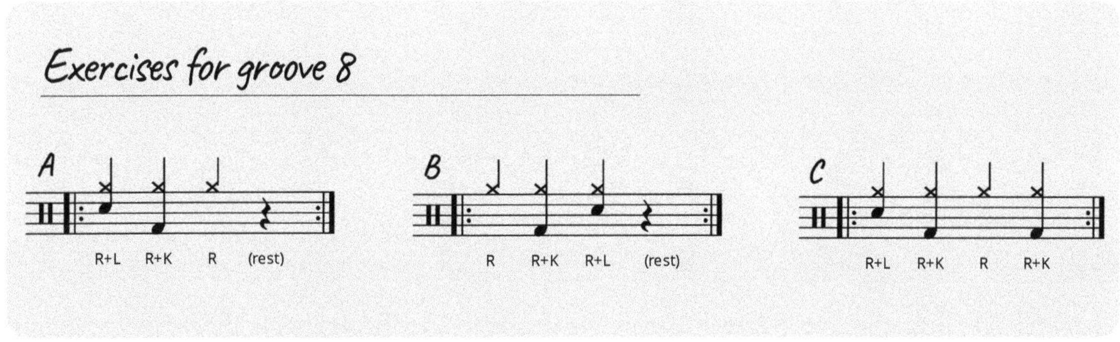
Exercises for groove 8
A
R+L R+K R (rest)
B
R R+K R+L (rest)
C
R+L R+K R R+K

8
1 2 - & (3) - & 4

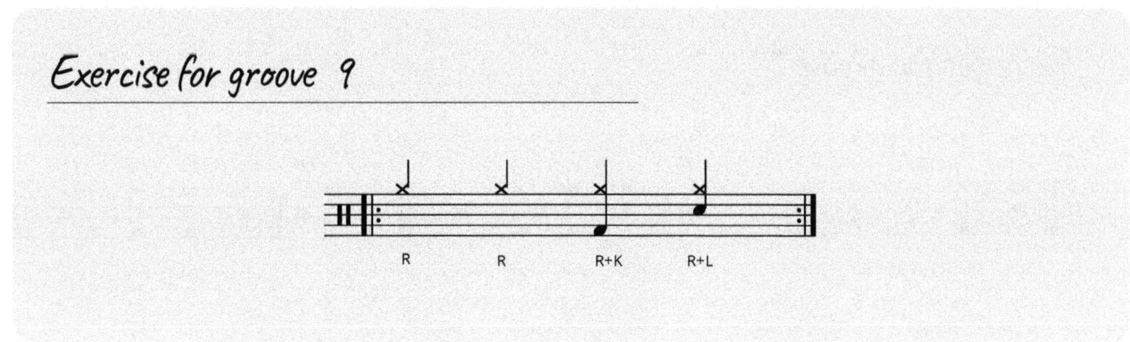
Exercise for groove 9
R
R
R+K
R+L

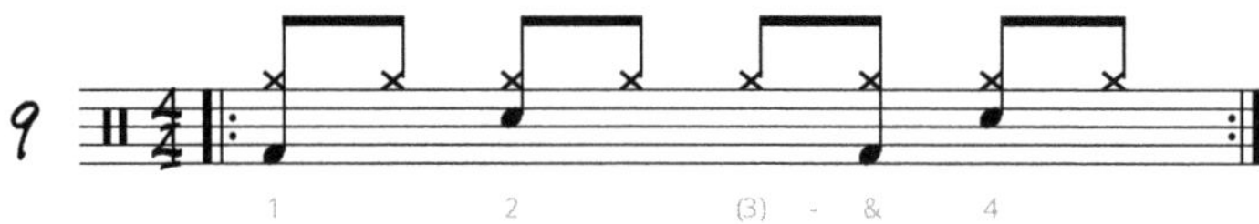
9
1
2
(3) - &
4

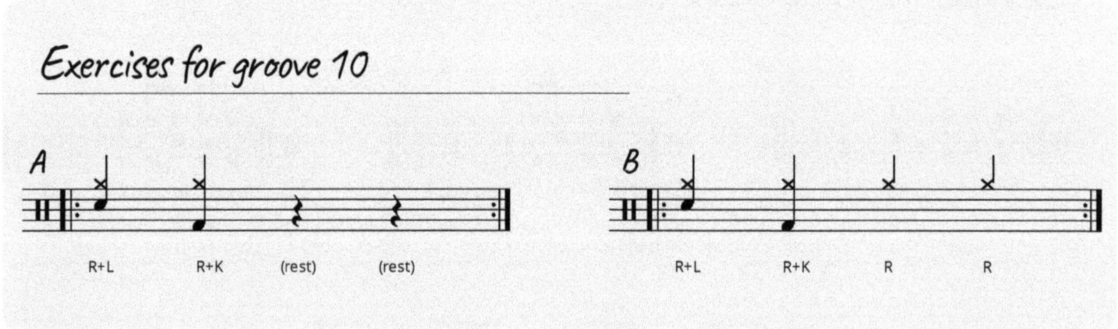
Exercises for groove 10
A
R+L
R+K
(rest)
(rest)
B
R+L
R+K
R
R

10
1
2 - &
(3)
4

4 - FILLS - *"1 e & a" fills*

As a drummer, besides grooves, you also play fills. Fills can be applied in different ways.
For example, to start or end a song, to fill up a space (fill in) or to connect two sections of a song, like the chorus with the verse.

In the next exercise you first play one bar with two eighths on each beat. Then one bar with four sixteenths on each beat. Every beat is played on a different drum.

FILL VARIATIONS

You are now going to combine the 8th and 16th figures. Every figure is played on a different drum.
You start on the snare and then go over the toms clockwise.

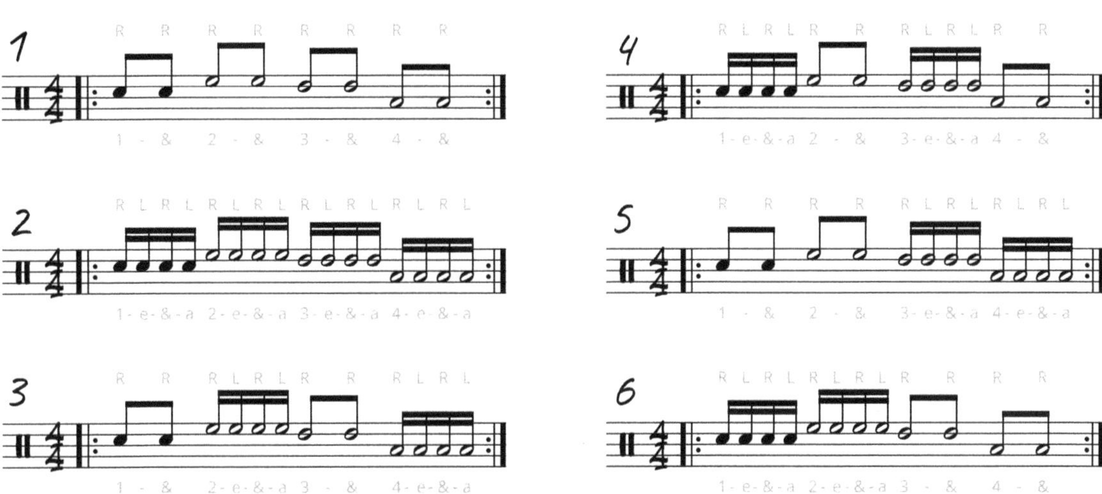

GROOVES WITH CRASH

We often play the crash on the first beat of the first groove after a fill and/or at the beginning of a series of grooves. We exchange the first hi-hat stroke with a stroke on the crash. In these exercises you learn to resume the groove smoothly after a stroke on the crash. The crash note has the same symbol (cross) as the hi-hat note but is written a little higher on the staff with a sight line.

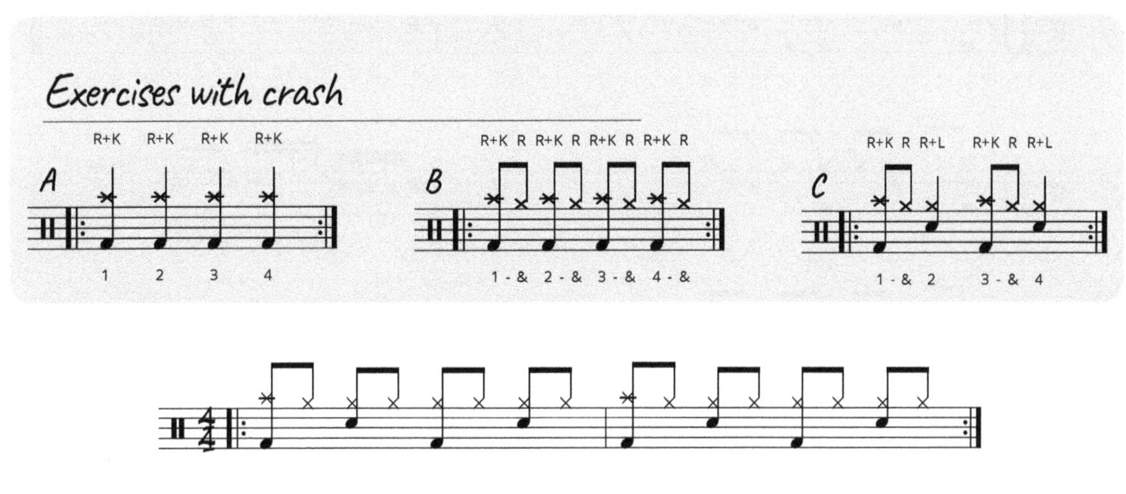

GROOVES AND FILLS

You are now going to combine the fills you have already learned in the fill variation with grooves. In these exercises you play a groove and then repeat it twice. The first groove starts with the crash on the first beat. With the two repetitions you play the hi-hat on the first beat. After the grooves you play the fill on the snare and toms. You also repeat this whole exercise at least twice. This way you learn to resume the groove after the fill in the same tempo.

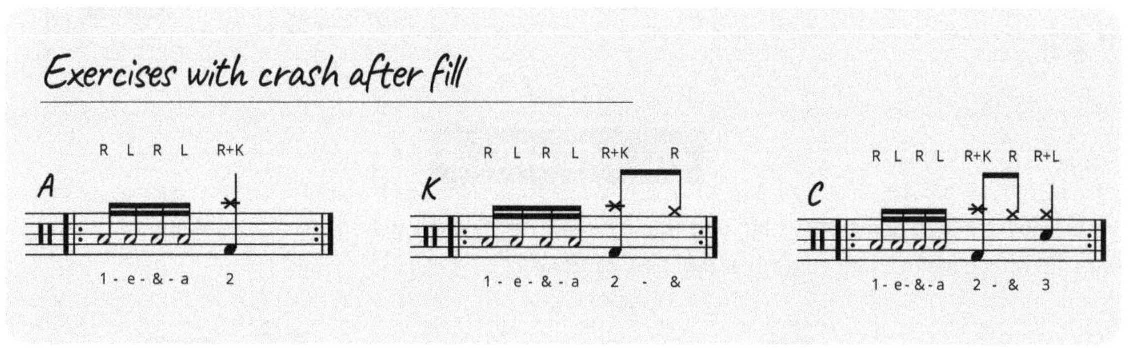

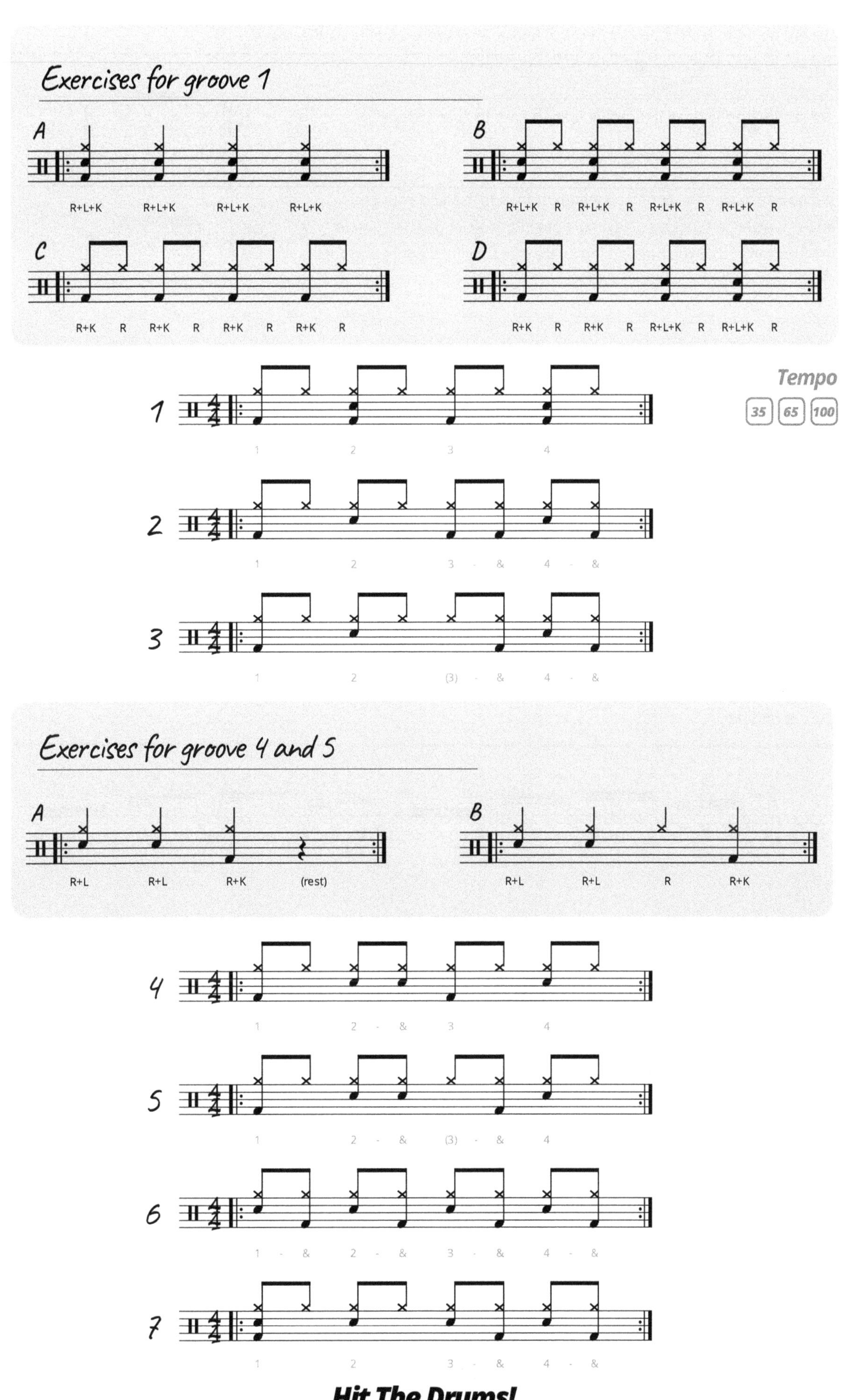
Exercises for groove 1
A
R+L+K R+L+K R+L+K R+L+K
B
R+L+K R R+L+K R R+L+K R R+L+K R
C
R+K R R+K R R+K R R+K R
D
R+K R R+K R R+L+K R R+L+K R
1
1 2 3 4
Tempo
35 65 100
2
1 2 3 - & 4 - &
3
1 2 (3) - & 4 - &
Exercises for groove 4 and 5
A
R+L R+L R+K (rest)
B
R+L R+L R R+K
4
1 2 - & 3 4
5
1 2 - & (3) - & 4
6
1 - & 2 - & 3 - & 4 - &
7
1 2 3 - & 4 - &

6 - FILLS - *"1 - & a" fills*

We are going to learn a new rhythmical figure. Play the exercises on the snare.
Try to say the new figure out loud while you play it.

We start with the base figure that is made out of four sixteenths.

We now remove the second sixteenth note. It is marked with grey and is written in brackets. Play this note in the air or on the edge of the first tom. Now you hear on the snare what the new figure sounds like.

The rhythmical figure is written as followed: one eighth note and two sixteenth notes on the end.

Try to play the figure in sequence on each drum of your drum set.

In the next exercise you play the base figure on each beat in the first bar and the new figure on each beat in the second bar.

FILL VARIATIONS

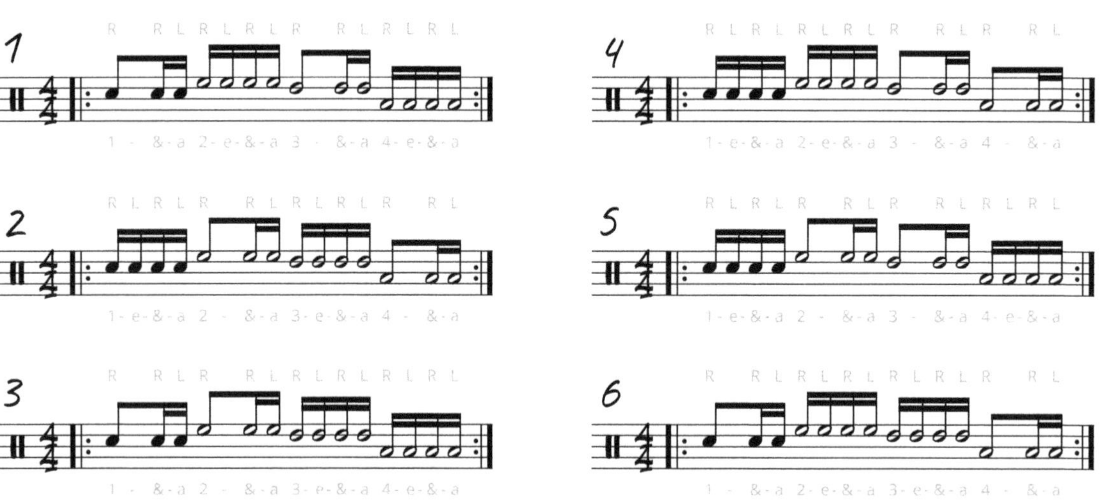

6 - FILLS - *"1 - & a" fills*

GROOVES AND FILLS

Tempo

45 65 100

7 - GROOVES - *2 bar eighth note hi-hat grooves*

The next grooves are divided into two bars. They are common in songs, because they make the groove less repetitive. Try to play the groove from memory after you have repeated it a couple of times.

8 - FILLS - *"1 e &" fills*

We are going to learn a new rhythmical figure. Play the exercises on the snare. Try to say the new figure out loud while you play it.

We start with the base figure that is made out of four sixteenths.

We now remove the fourth sixteenth note. It is marked with grey and is written in brackets. Play this note in the air or on the edge of the first tom. Now you hear on the snare what the new figure sounds like.

The rhythmical figure is written as followed: two sixteenth notes and one eighth note on the end.

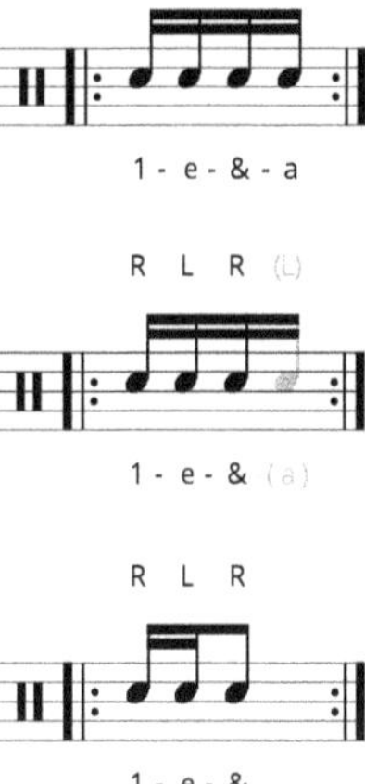

Try to play the figure in sequence on each drum of your drum set.

In the next exercise you play the base figure on each beat in the first bar and the new figure on each beat in the second bar.

FILL VARIATIONS

8 - FILLS - "1 e &" fills

GROOVES AND FILLS

Tempo

45 65 100

9 - **GROOVES** - *Quarter note hi-hat*

A groove played with quarter notes on the hi-hat create a powerful sound on the beat. These grooves are perfect for songs with a high tempo. You play less notes on the hi-hat, which makes it easier to keep going. It helps to make the hi-hat stroke bigger by raising your arm higher. Try to keep the hi-hat more open for a heavier sound or play the right hand on the bell of the ride (the bulge in the middle of the cymbal).

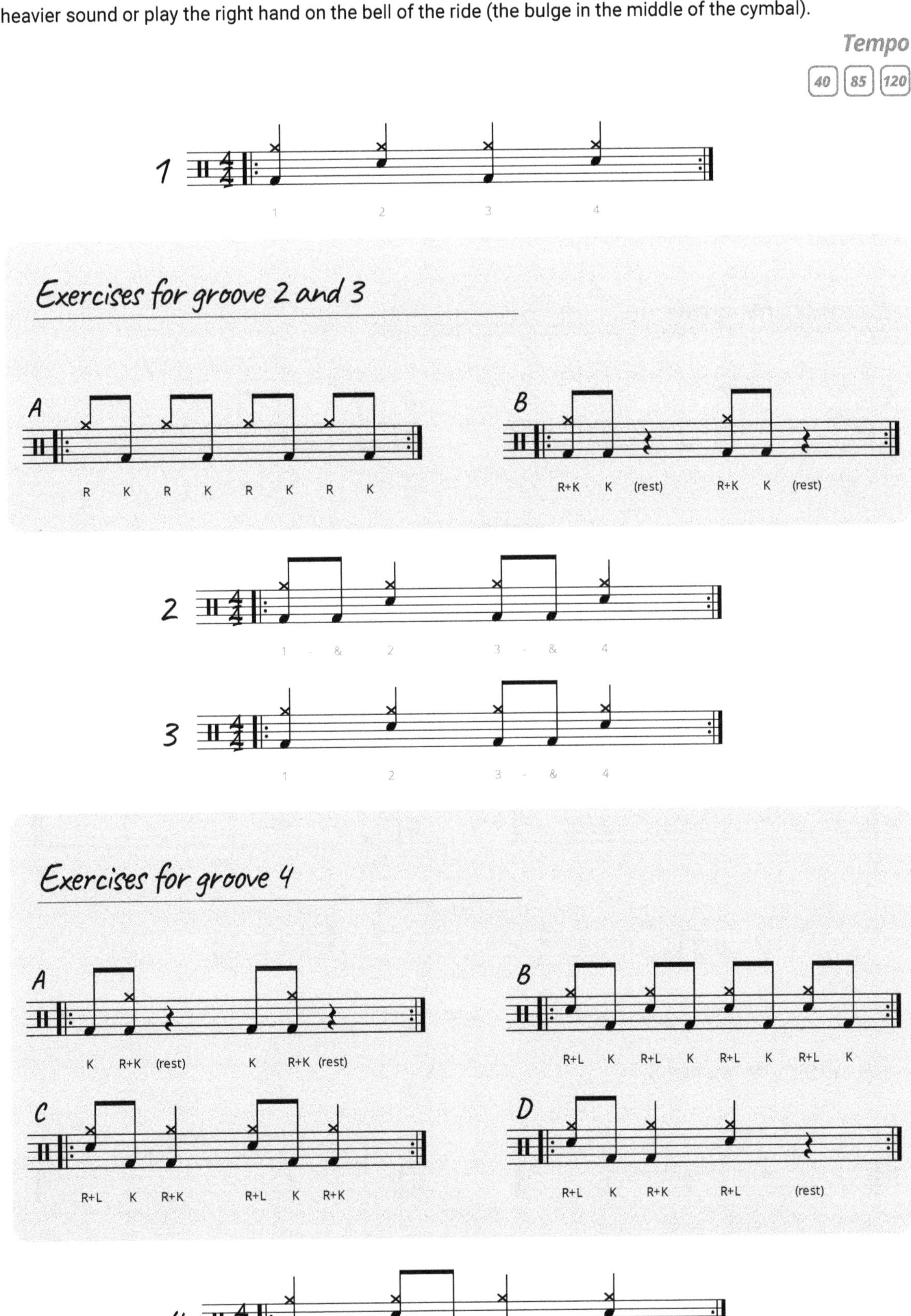

Exercises for groove 5
A
R+K K R+L (rest) (rest)
B
C
5
1 - & 2 - & 3 4
Exercises for groove 6
A
B
6
1 2 - & (3) 4
Exercises for groove 7
A
B
7
1 2 (3) - & 4
Exercises for groove 8
A
R+K R+L K (rest) (rest)
B
R+K R+L K R K (rest)
8
1 2 - & (3) - & 4

10 - FILLS - *Short fills starting on four*

You have been playing fills of four beats until now. We often play shorter fills of one or two beats in songs. In this way we are giving the other musicians in the band some more space. In these exercises you play the short fill at the end of the bar on the fourth beat.

Tempo

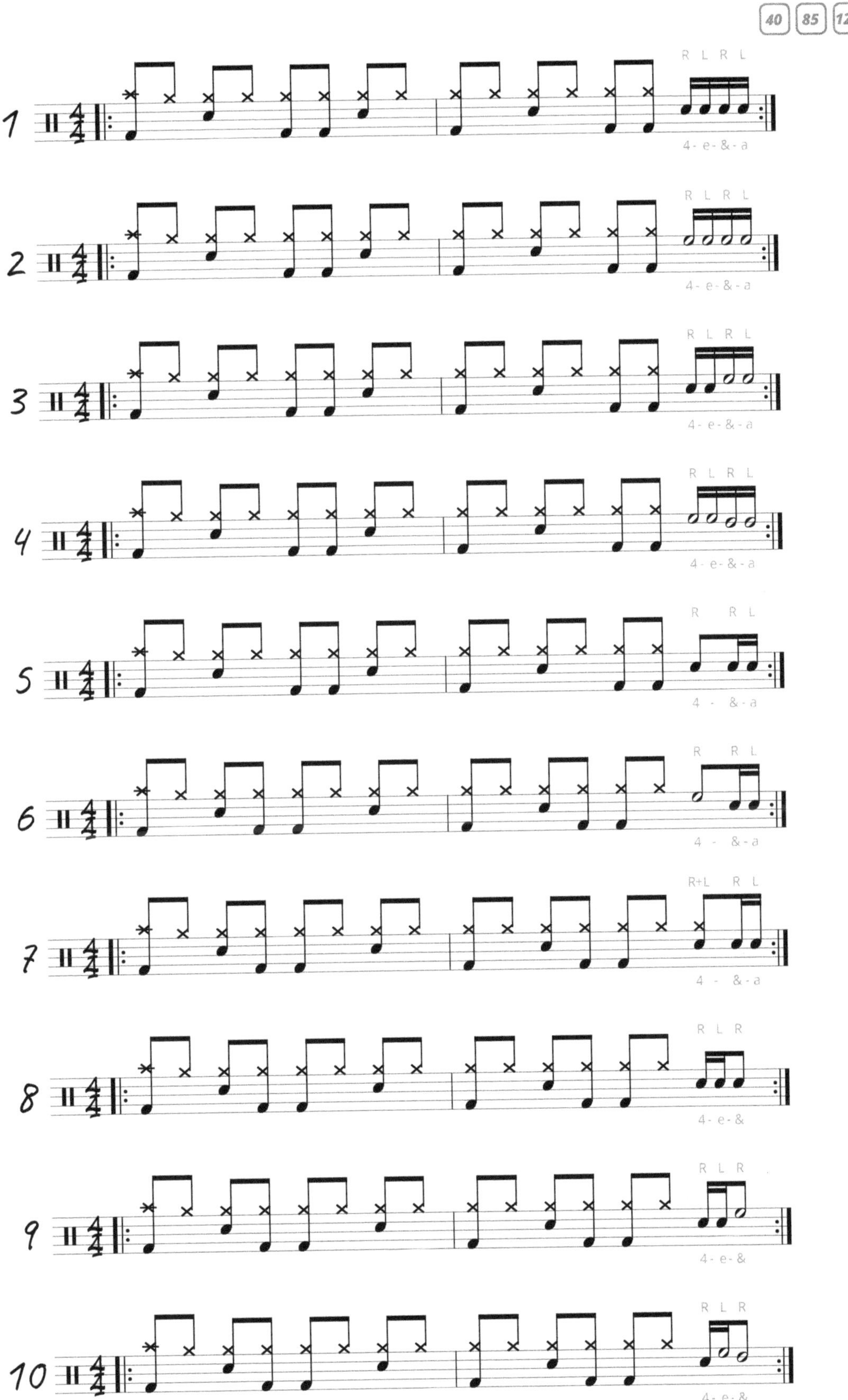

11 - GROOVES - *Sixteenth note hi-hat (RLRL) #1*

You have only been using the right hand on the hi-hat until now. Now we will be using both hands.
Play the strokes alternately (RLRL) and make sure these strokes sound regular.
The snare is played on the second and fourth beat with the right hand.

Tempo

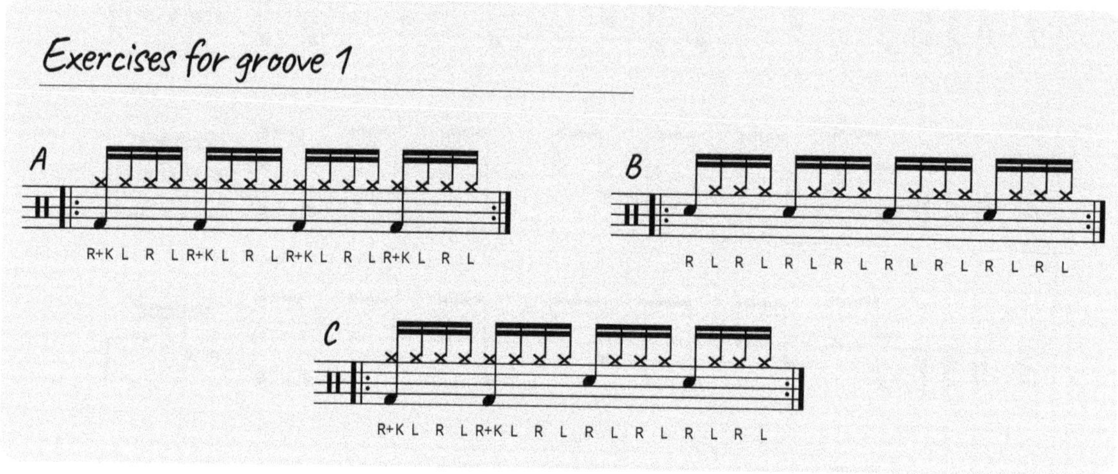

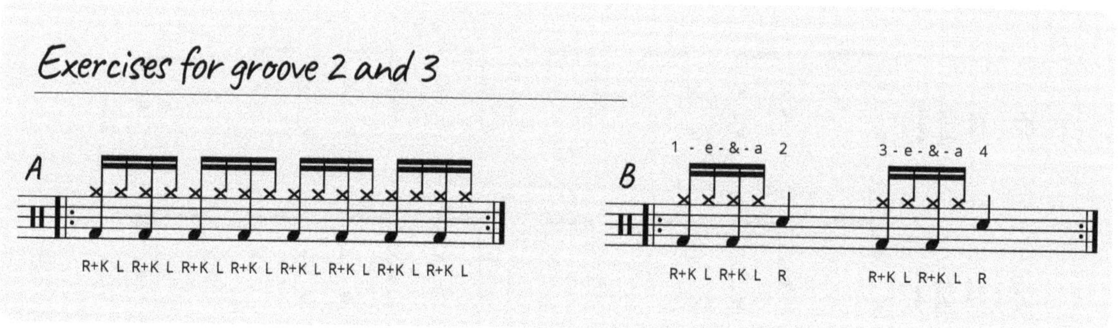

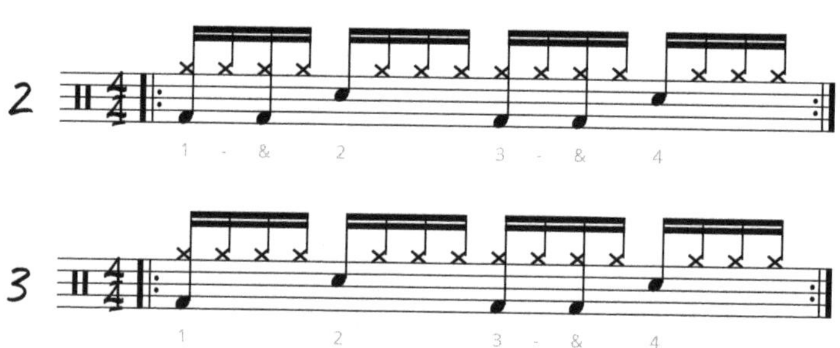

Exercises for groove 4

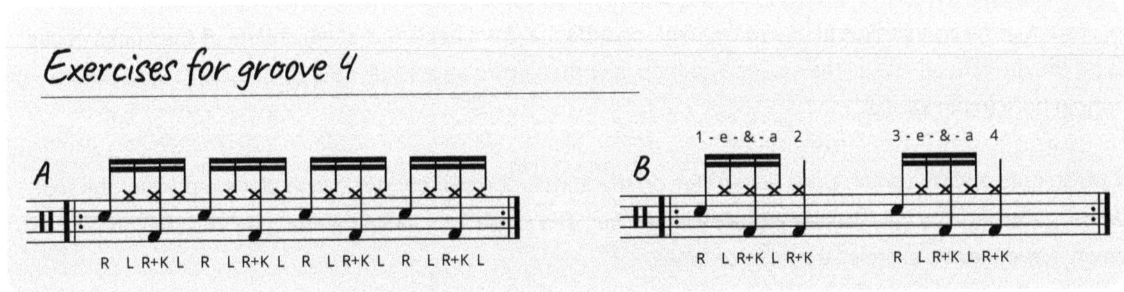

Exercises for groove 5 till 7

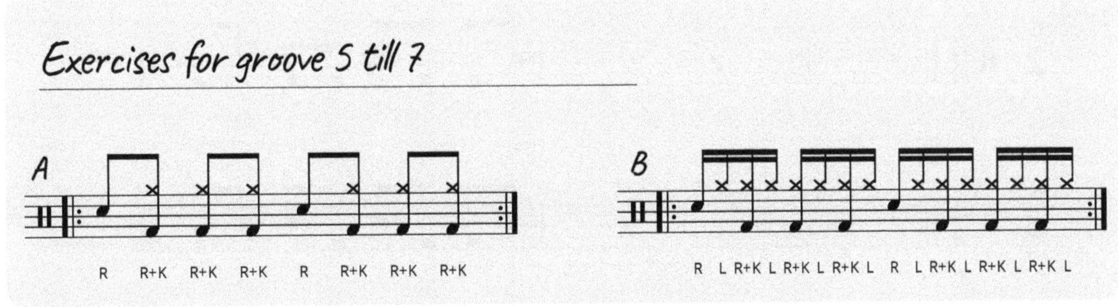

Exercises for groove 8

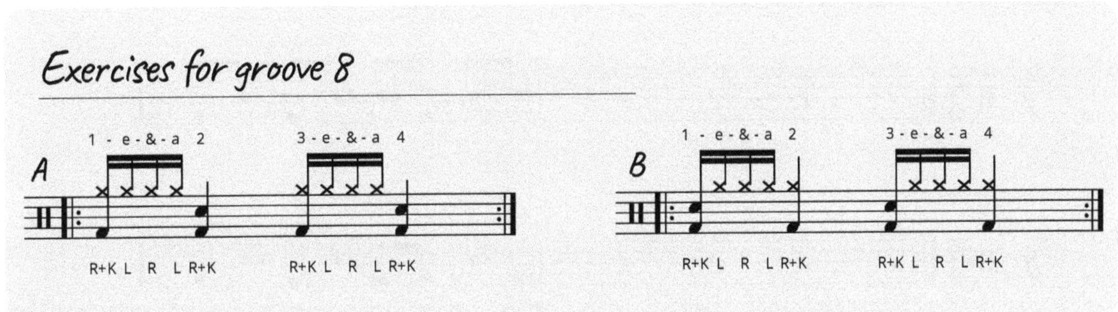

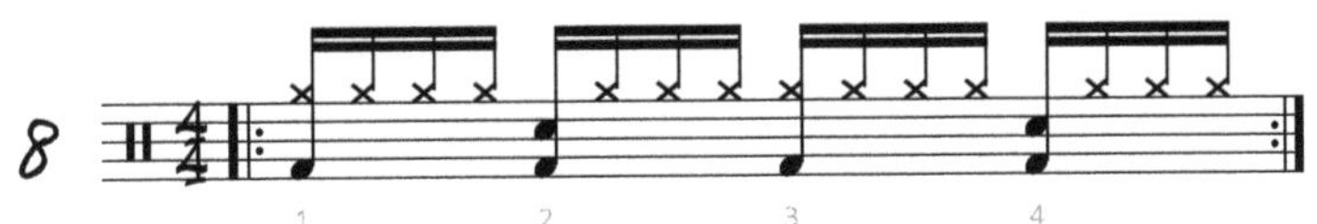

12 - FILLS - *Flam fills*

A flam consists out of two strokes. You play a somewhat softer stroke (first stroke) right before the main stroke. You play the two strokes in one movement towards the drum head, out of which one of the sticks needs to hit the drum head just a little earlier. The flam is written down as a small note (first stroke) right before a normal note (main stroke).

A crash note and four slash signs are written on the staff in the first bar. The slash signs represent the four beats in the bar. You have to play a groove in this bar. The crash note indicates that you start the groove with a crash. Repeat every exercise a couple of times.

Also try to play the flam strokes on different toms.

13 - GROOVES - *Offbeat*

In offbeat/upbeat grooves we play the hi-hat only after the beat on the second eighth note, so on "&".
It helps to make the hi-hat stroke bigger by lifting up your arm higher.

Tempo

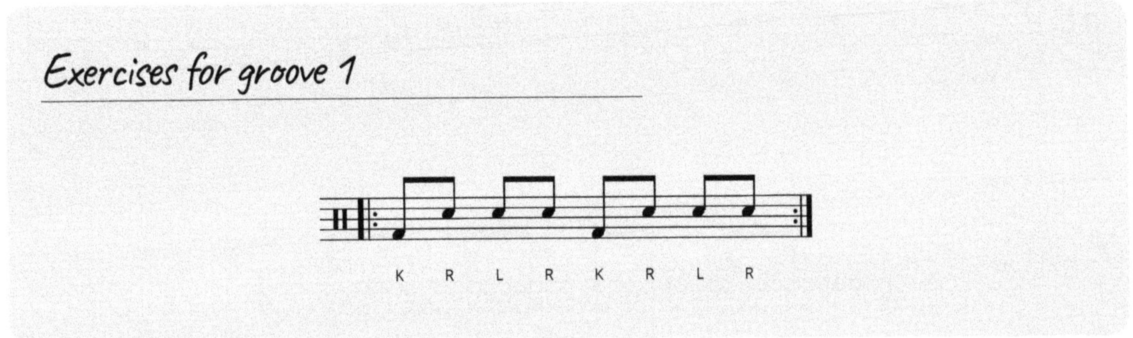

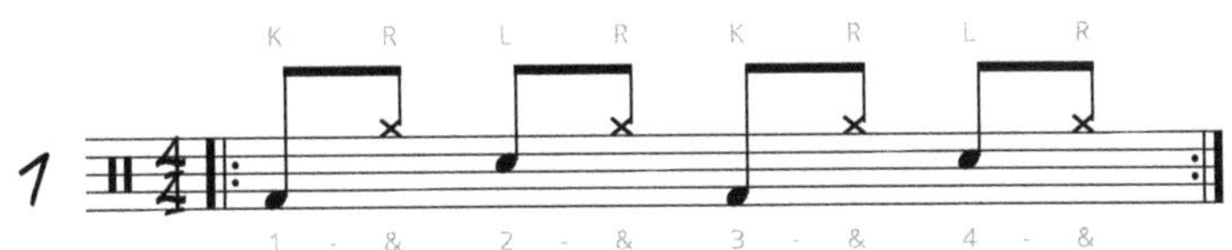

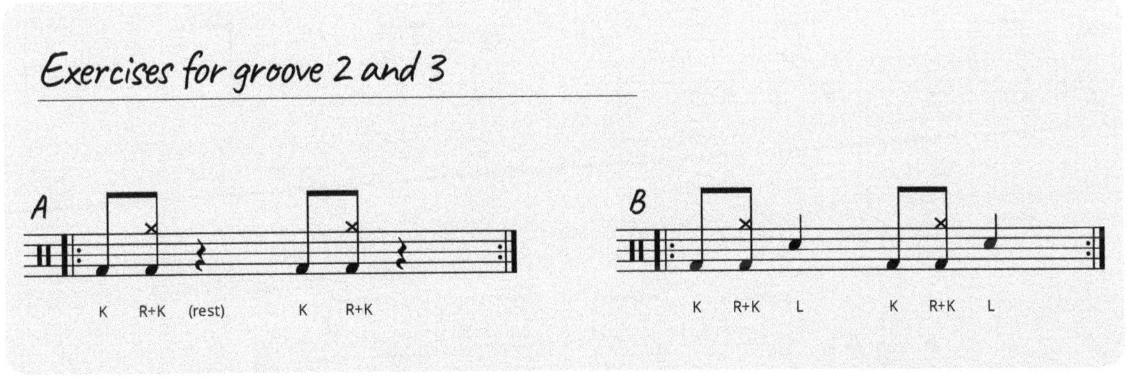

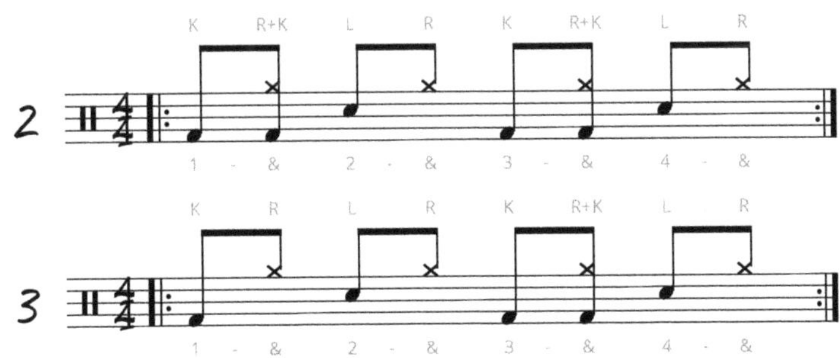

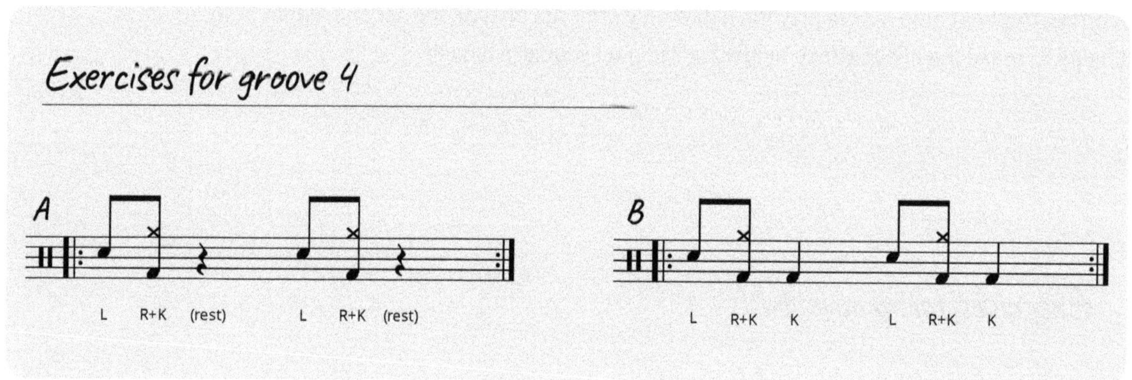
Exercises for groove 4
A
L R+K (rest) L R+K (rest)
B
L R+K K L R+K K

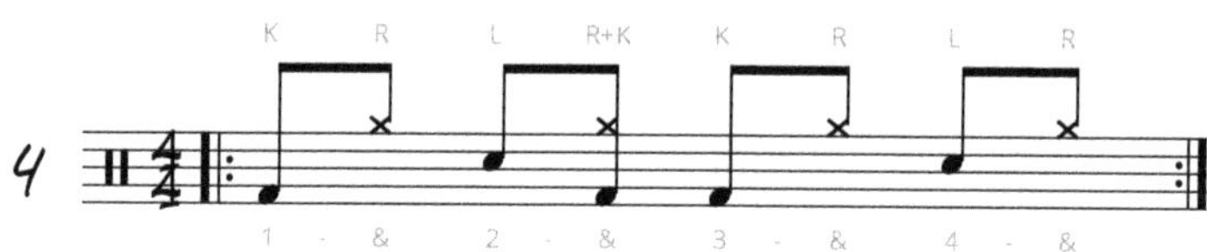
K R L R+K K R L R
4
1 - & 2 - & 3 - & 4 - &

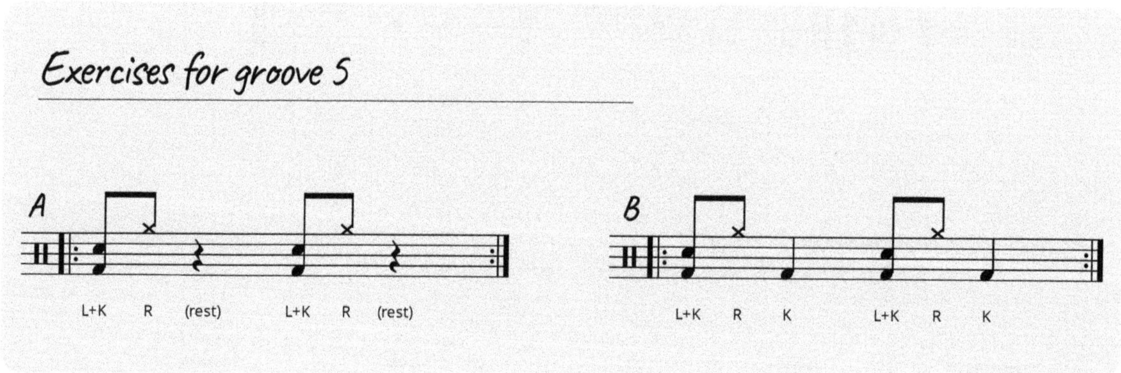
Exercises for groove 5
A
L+K R (rest) L+K R (rest)
B
L+K R K L+K R K

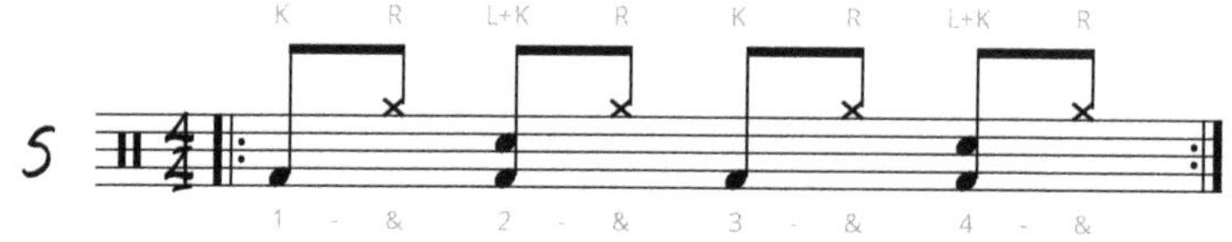
K R L+K R K R L+K R
5
1 - & 2 - & 3 - & 4 - &

14 - FILLS - *Crescendo fills*

A crescendo or build-fill is a simple but powerful drum fill. You start playing it softly and then you gradually increase the volume. You can see the "crescendo" symbol underneath each fill.

15 - GROOVES - *Open hi-hat #1*

You will start using your left foot for the first time to operate the hi-hat pedal. The note with the little cross and an "O" above indicates that you need to play an open hi-hat. You get an open hi-hat sound when you raise the left foot and then hit the hi-hat. The note with the little cross underneath on the staff indicates that you need to keep the hi-hat pedal pressed to play a closed hi-hat note.

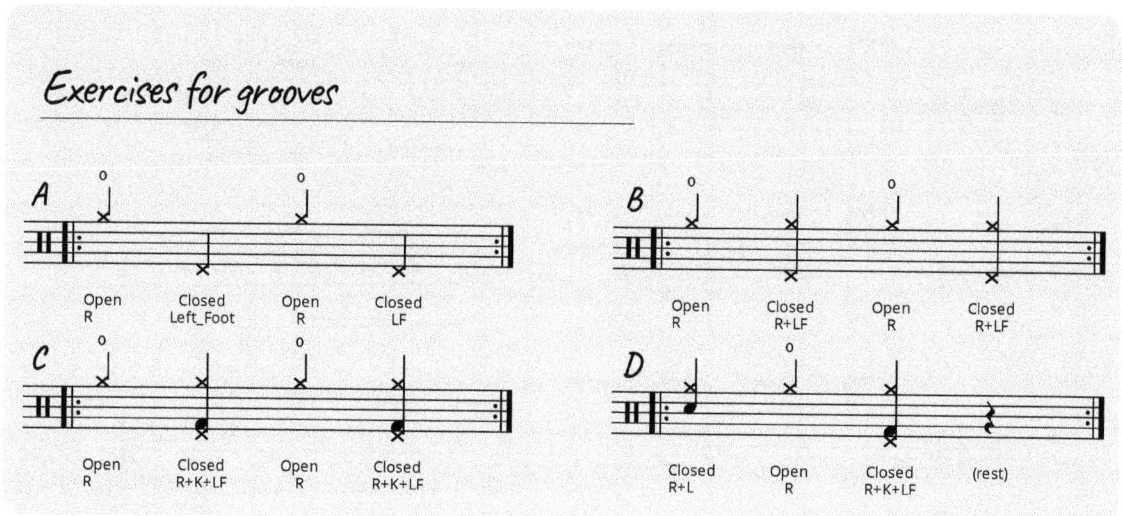

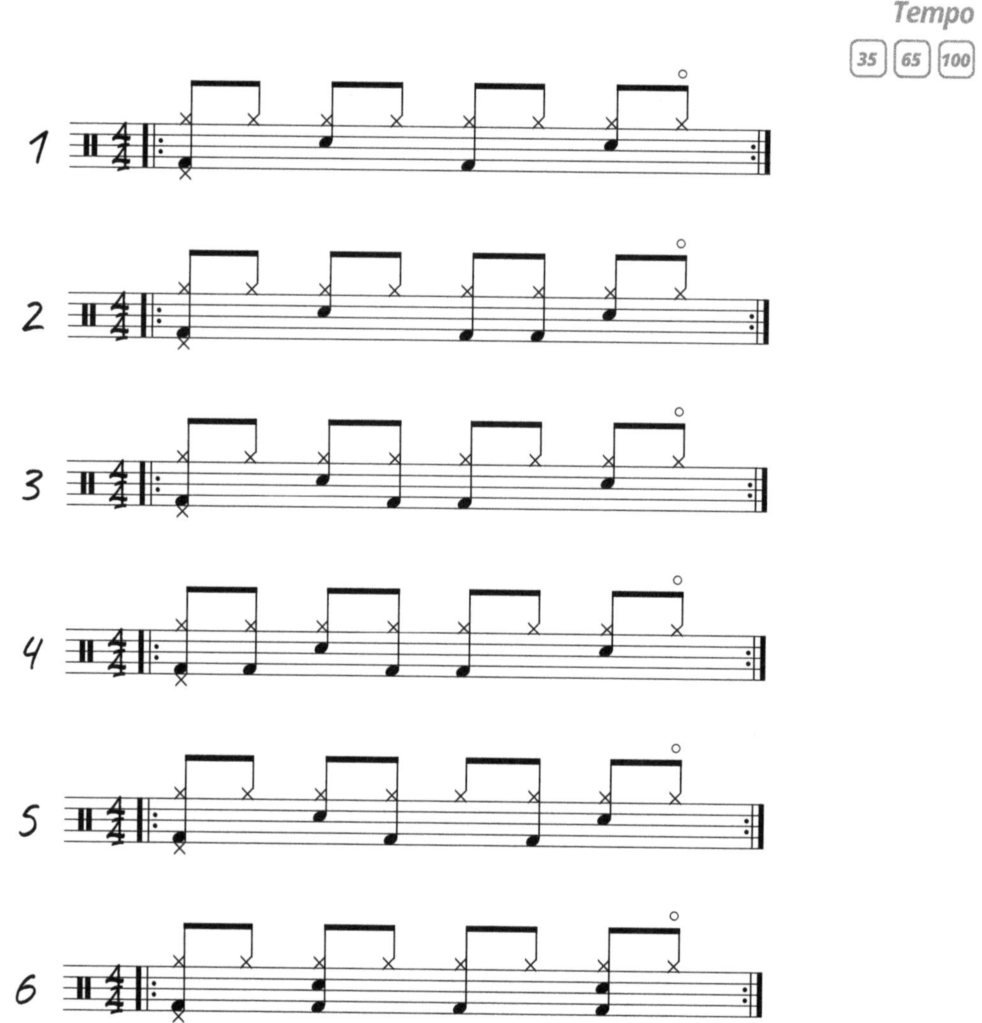

16 - GROOVES - *Sixteenth note hi-hat (RRRR) #1*

These grooves look like the ones from chapter 11, but there is a small difference. The hi-hat is now being played with one hand instead of with both hands. You play the hi-hat together with the snare on the back beats (second and fourth beat).

Tempo

17 - FILLS - *Short fills starting on three #1*

The exercises consist out of 2 bars. In the first bar you play a groove. In the second bar you keep playing the groove for another 2 beats, after which you start the short fill on the third beat.

Tempo

40 85 120

***17 - FILLS** - Short fills starting on three #1*

Tempo

40 | 85 | 120

18 - GROOVES - *Open hi-hat #2*

In these grooves you close the open hi-hat on the moment you play the snare.

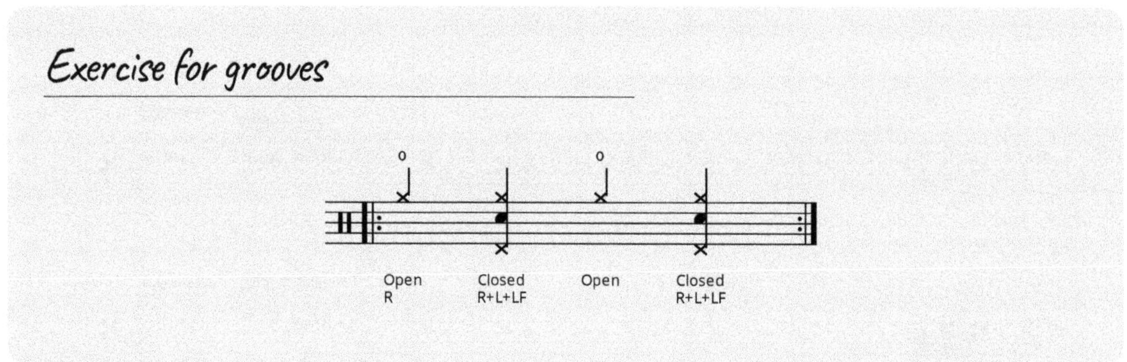

19 - FILLS - *Short fills starting on three #2*

In this chapter we play short fills of 2 beats.
In exercise 11 until 20 we start the fill with a kick drum and hi-hat.

Tempo

40 85 120

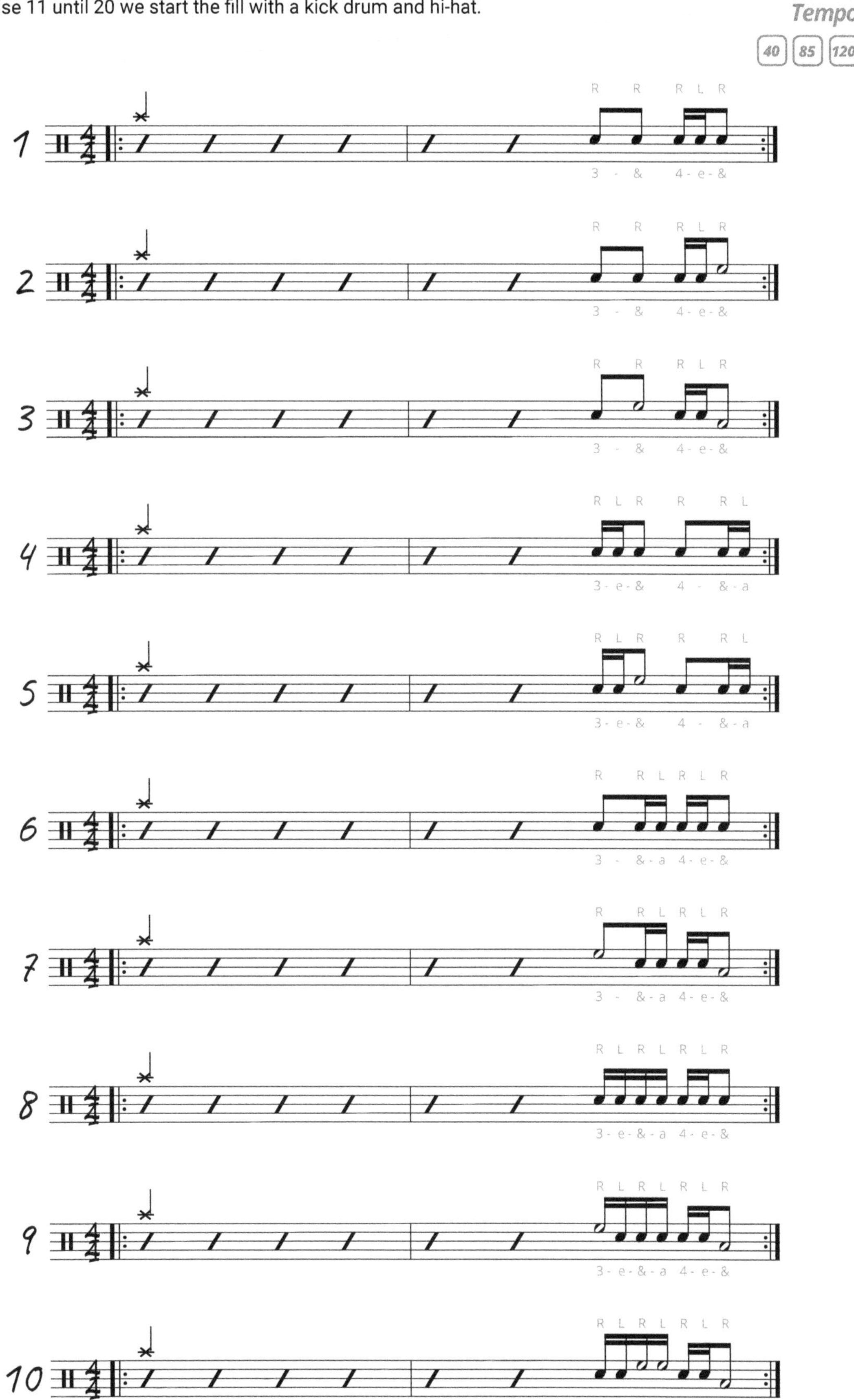

19 - FILLS - *Short fills starting on three #2*

20 - GROOVES - *Crash accents #1*

As a drummer we often support accents in the parts of other instruments. We emphasize certain tones in the melody. We play usually play these accents on the crash cymbal in combination with the snare drum or kick drum.

Tempo

50 75 110

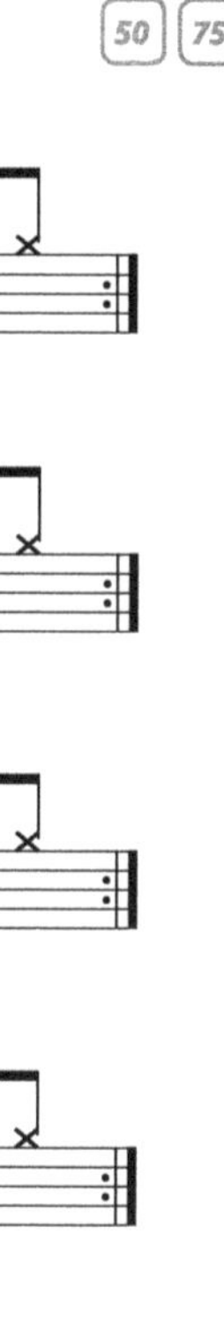

1

2

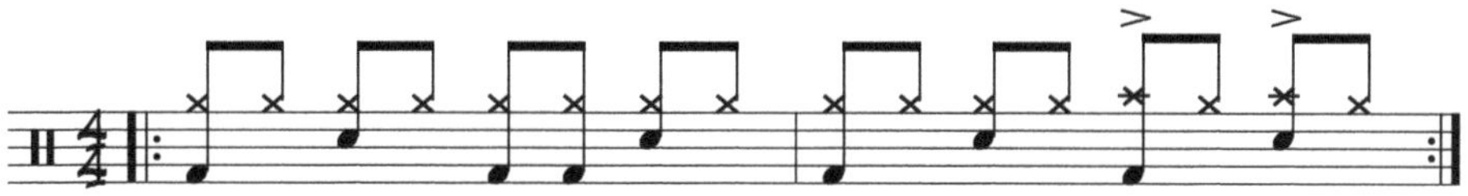

3

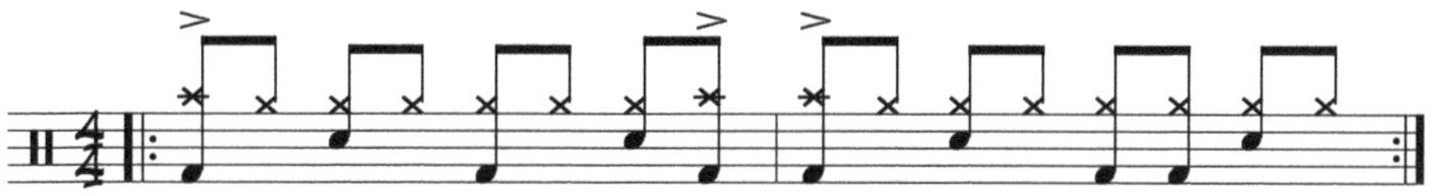

4

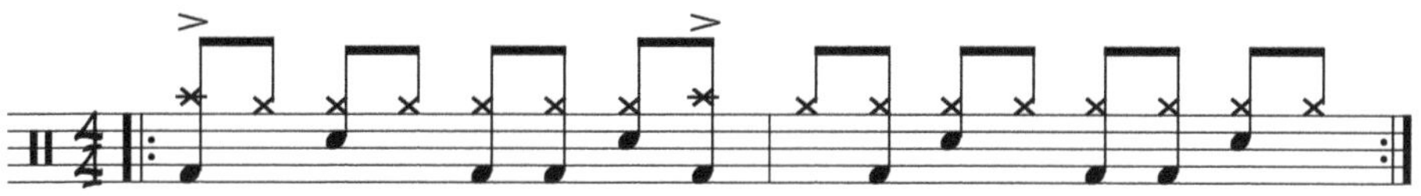

5

6

7

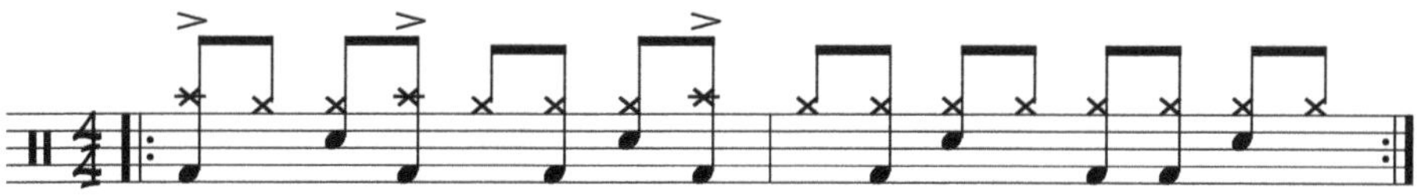

8

9

21 - FILLS - *"1 e - a" fills*

We are going to learn a new rhythmical figure. Play the exercises on the snare. Try to say the new figure out loud while you play it.

We start with the base figure that is made out of four sixteenths.

We now remove the third sixteenth note. It is marked with grey and is written in brackets. Play this note in the air or on the edge of the first tom. Now you hear on the snare what the new figure sounds like.

The rhythmical figure is written as followed: one sixteenth, one eighth and another one sixteenth on the end.

Try to play the figure in sequence on each drum of your drum set.

In the next exercise you play the base figure on each beat in the first bar and the new figure on each beat in the second bar.

FILL VARIATIONS

21 - FILLS - "1 e - a" fills

GROOVES WITH FILLS

Tempo

45 65 100

In this groove you play an open hi-hat while you play the kick drum. You close the open hi-hat on the moment you play the kick drum on the first beat.

Exercises for groove 1 till 3

A

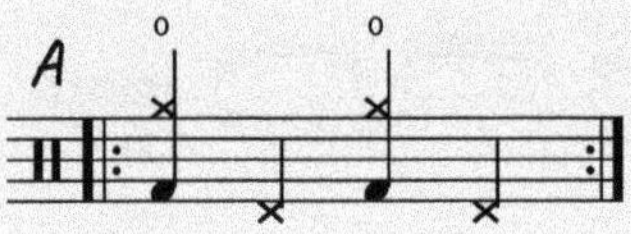

Open R+B | Closed LF | Open R+K | Closed LF

B

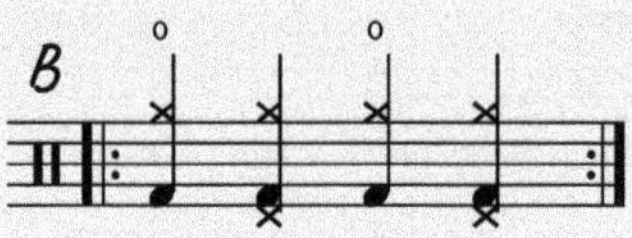

Open R+K | Closed R+K+LF | Open R+K | Closed R+K+LF

C

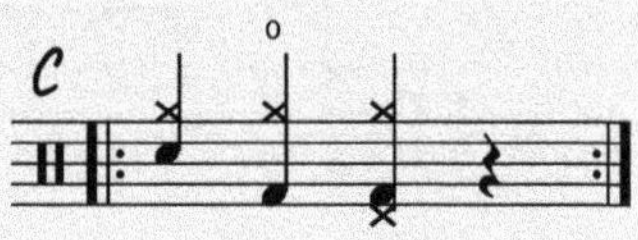

Closed R+L | Open R+K | Closed R+K+LF | (rest)

Tempo 35 65 100

1

2

3

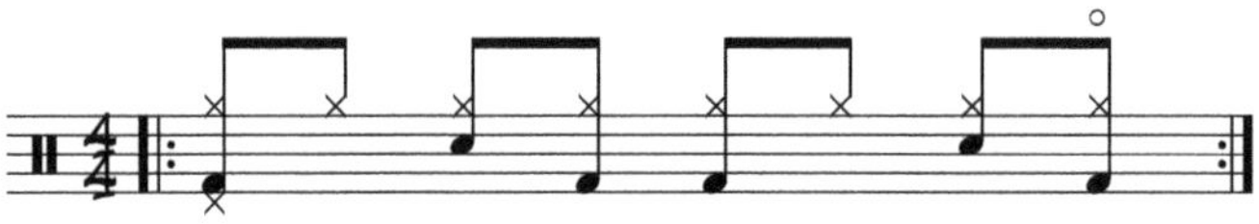

Exercises for groove 4 till 6

A

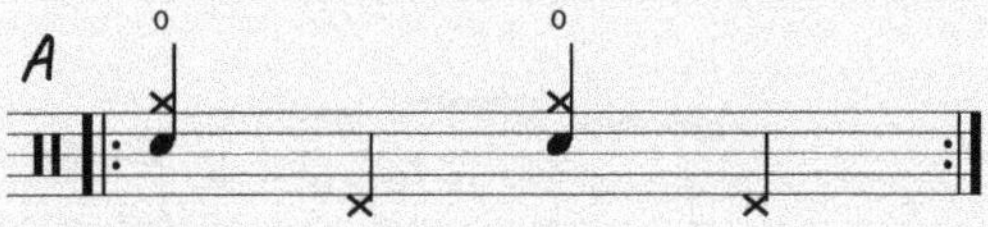

Open R+L | Closed LF | Open R+L | Closed LF

B

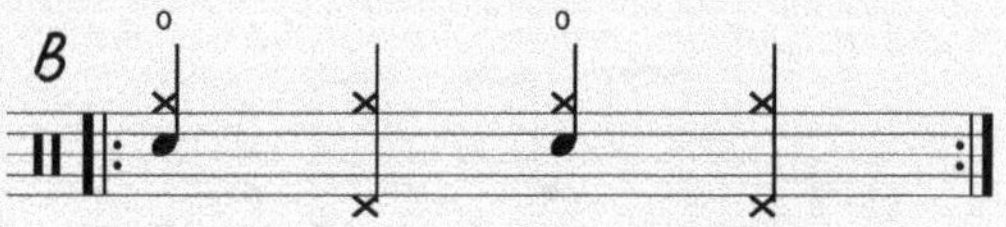

Open R+L | Closed R+LF | Open R+L | Closed R+LF

C

Open R+L | Closed R+K+LF | Open R+L | Closed R+K+LF

D

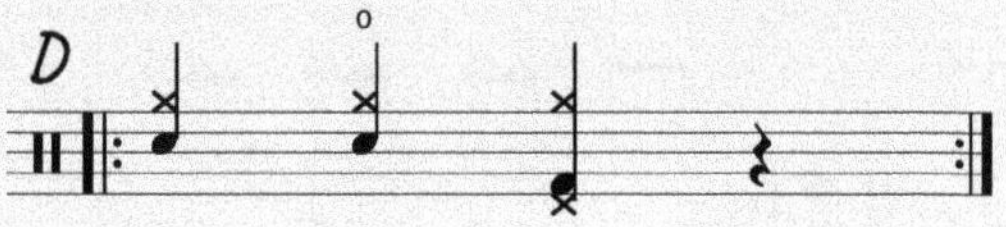

Closed R+L | Open R+L | Closed R+K+LF | (rest)

In the next groove we play the hi-hat open on the last snare drum.

23 - GROOVES - *Syncopated snare drum #1*

In these grooves you play a sixteenth note on the snare drum with your left hand in between the hi-hat notes.

Exercises for grooves

A

R L R L R L R L

B

R L R+K R L R+K

C

R+L R L R+K (rest)

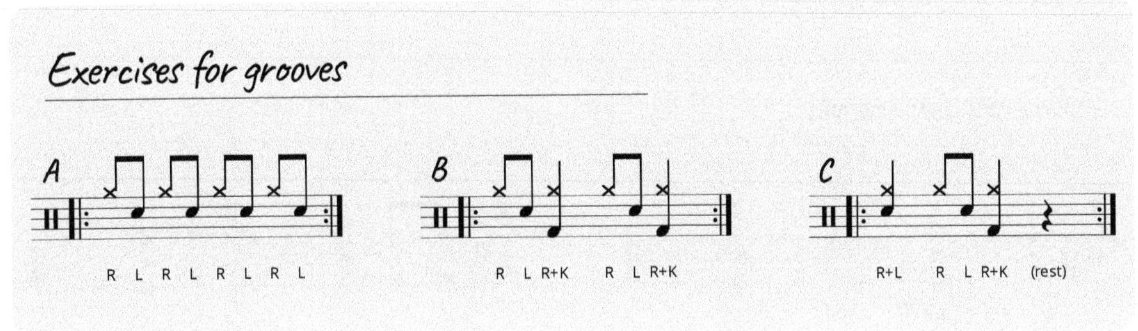

Tempo

35 65 100

1

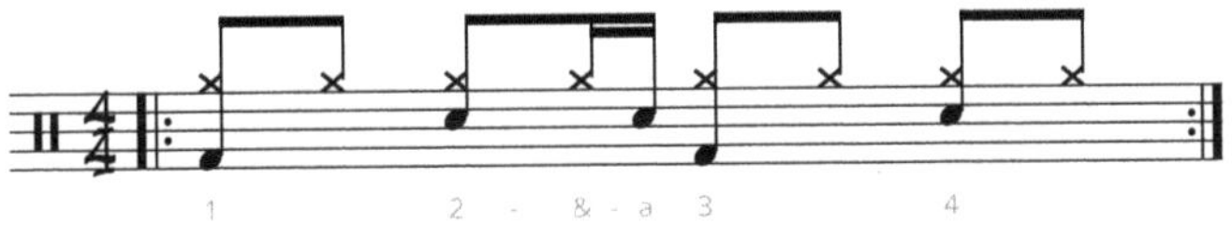

1 2 - & - a 3 4

2

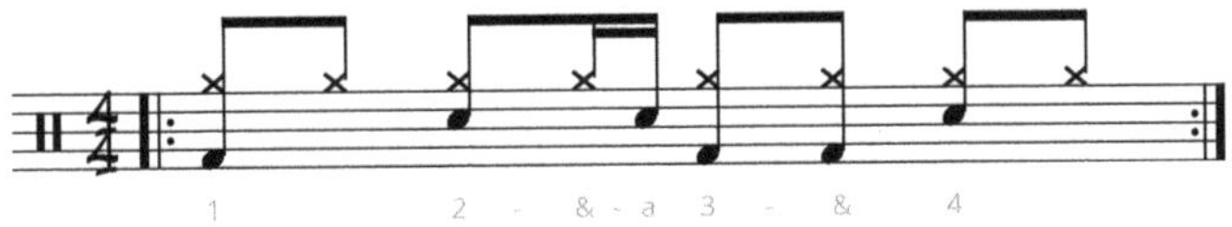

1 2 - & - a 3 - & 4

3

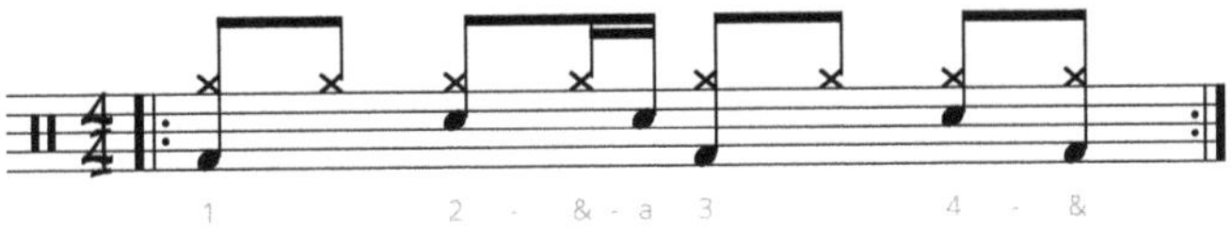

1 2 - & - a 3 4 - &

4

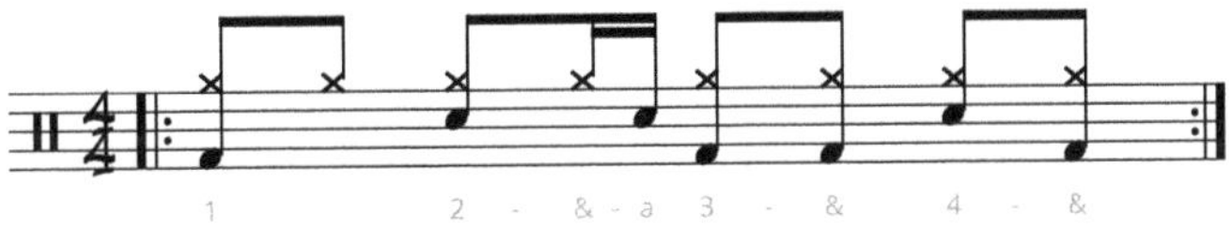

1 2 - & - a 3 - & 4 - &

5

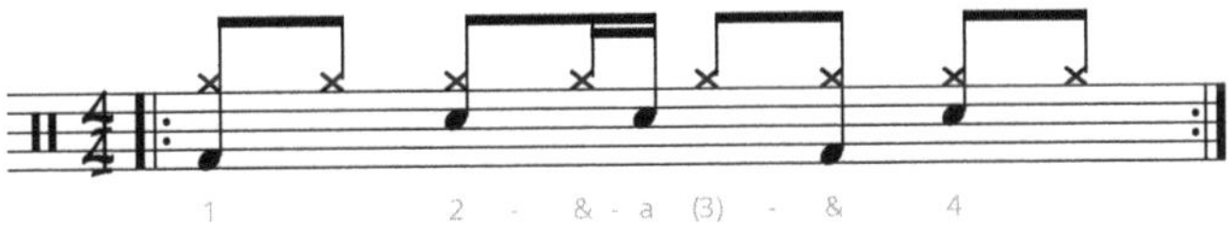

1 2 - & - a (3) - & 4

6

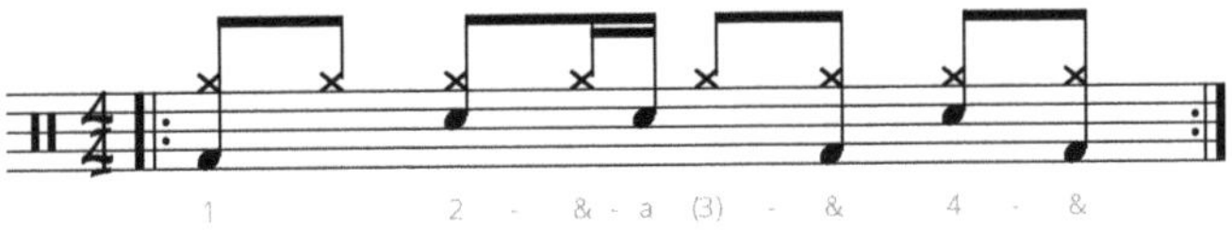

1 2 - & - a (3) - & 4 - &

7

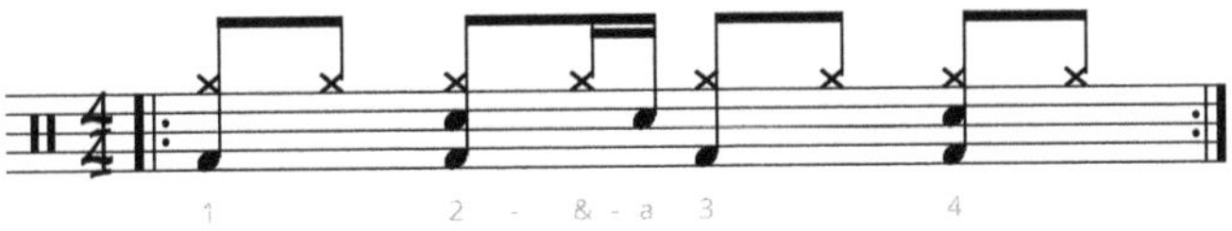

1 2 - & - a 3 4

8

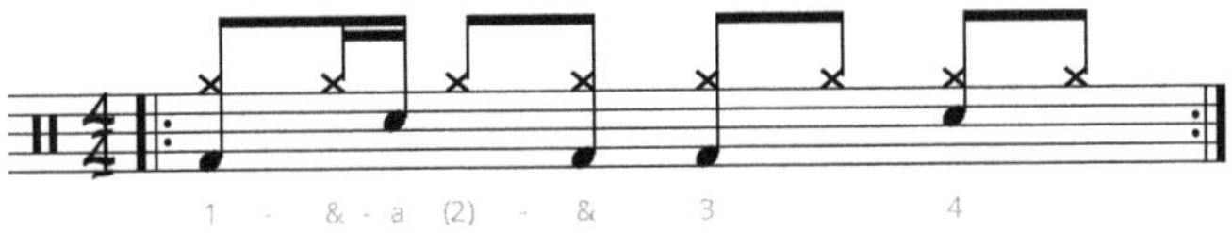

1 - & - a (2) - & 3 4

9

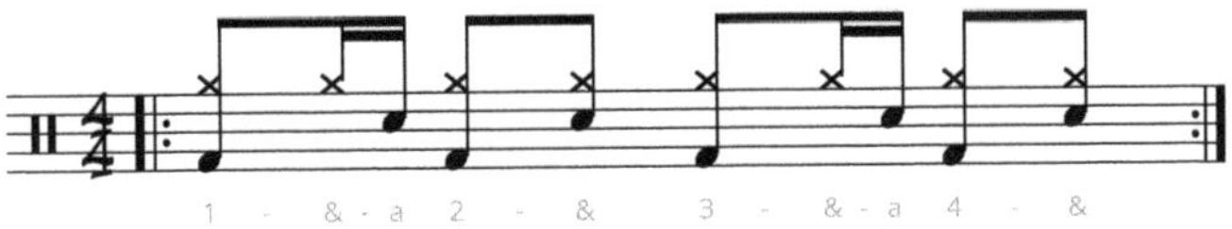

1 - & - a 2 - & 3 - & - a 4 - &

24 - GROOVES - Open hi-hat #4

In these grooves you play an open hi-hat on "3-and" while you play the bass drum. You close the open hi-hat on the stroke of the snare drum.

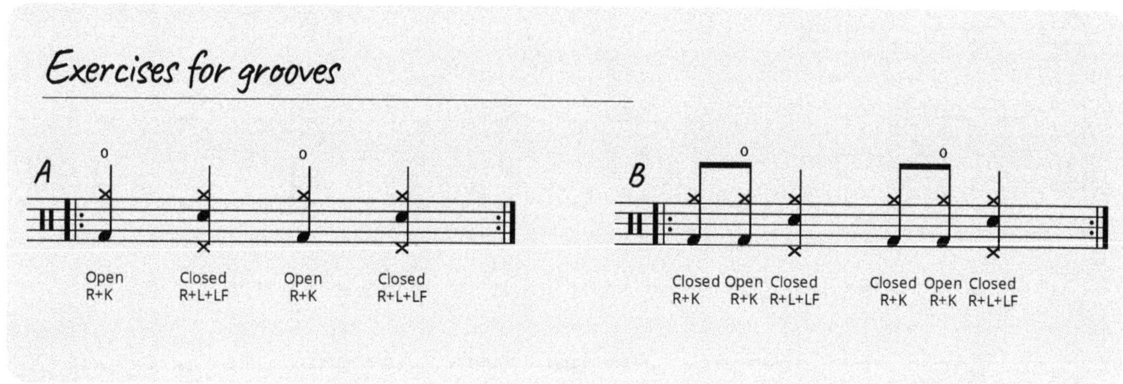

Tempo

35 65 100

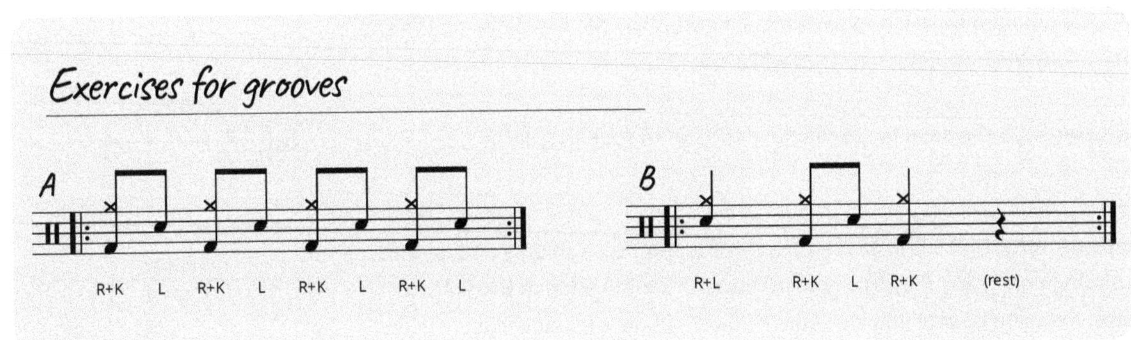

Tempo

35 65 100

26 - FILLS - "(1) e & a" fills

We are going to learn a new rhythmical figure. Play the exercises on the snare. Try to say the new figure out loud while you play it.

We start with the base figure that is made out of four sixteenths.

R L R L

1 - e - & - a

We now remove the first sixteenth note. It is marked with grey and is written in brackets. Play this note in the air or on the edge of the first tom. Now you hear on the snare what the new figure sounds like.

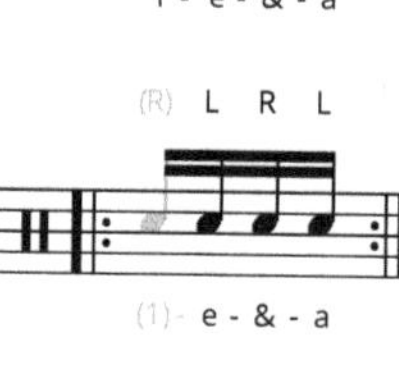

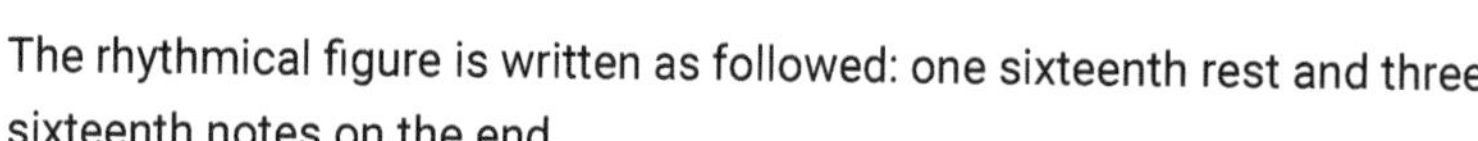

The rhythmical figure is written as followed: one sixteenth rest and three sixteenth notes on the end.

Try to play the figure in sequence on each drum of your drum set.

In the next exercise you play the base figure on each beat in the first bar and the new figure on each beat in the second bar.

FILL VARIATIONS

GROOVES AND FILLS

Exercises for groove 1 till 5

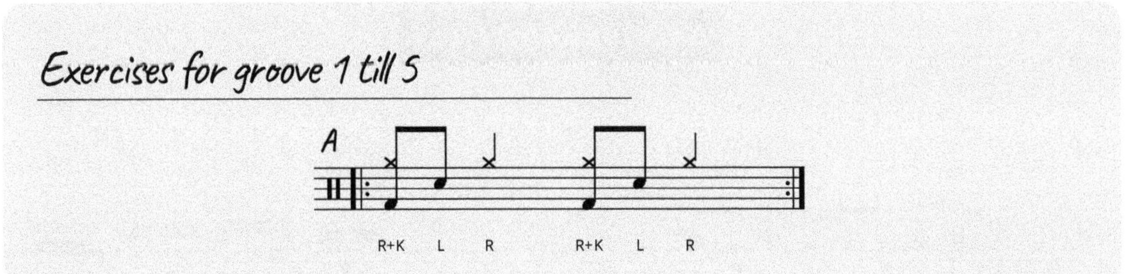

Tempo

35 65 100

Exercise for groove 6 and 7

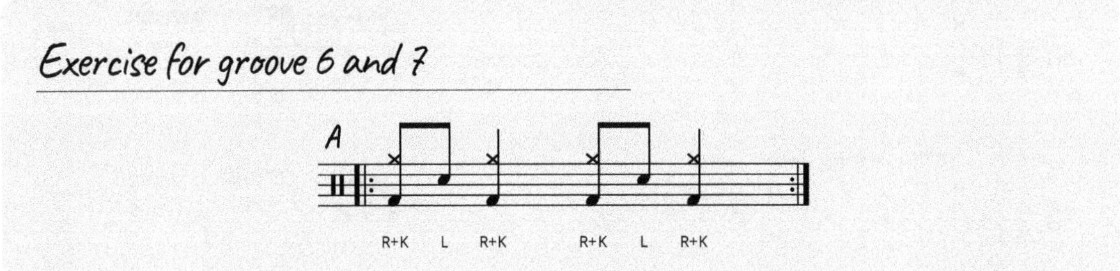

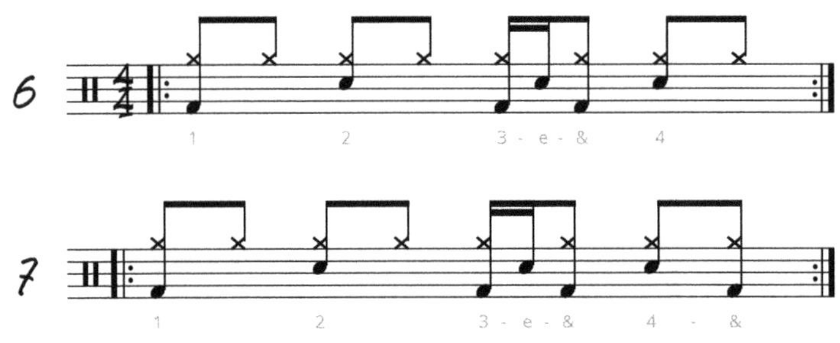

28 - FILLS - *"(1) e &" fills*

We are going to learn a new rhythmical figure. Play the exercises on the snare. Try to say the new figure out loud while you play it.

We start with the base figure that is made out of four sixteenths.

R L R L

1 - e - & - a

We now remove the first and last sixteenth note. These are marked with grey and are written in brackets. Play these notes in the air or on the edge of the first tom. Now you hear on the snare what the new figure sounds like.

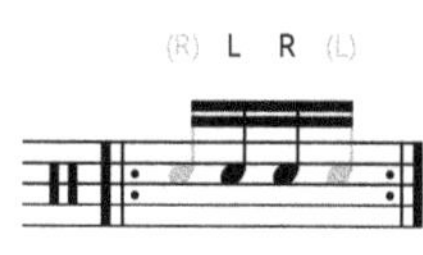

The rhythmical figure is written as followed: one sixteenth rest, one sixteenth note and one eighth note on the end.

Try to play the figure in sequence on each drum of your drum set.

In the next exercise you play the base figure on each beat in the first bar and the new figure on each beat in the second bar.

FILL VARIATIONS

GROOVES AND FILLS

Tempo

45 65 100

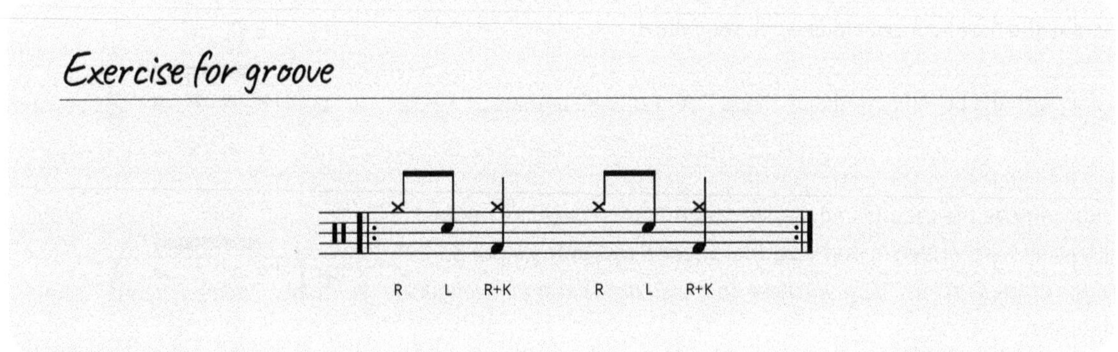
Exercise for groove
R L R+K R L R+K

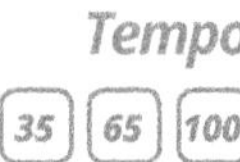
Tempo
35
65
100

1
1 2 (3) - e - & 4
2
1 - & 2 (3) - e - & 4
3
1 2 - & (3) - e - & 4
4
1 2 - & (3) - e - & 4 - &

30 - FILLS - "1 - - a" fills

We are going to learn a new rhythmical figure. Play the exercises on the snare.
Try to say the new figure out loud while you play it.

We start with the base figure that is made out of four sixteenths.

We now remove the second and third sixteenth note. These are marked with grey and are written in brackets. Play these notes in the air or on the edge of the first tom. Now you hear on the snare what the new figure sounds like.

The rhythmical figure is written as followed: one dotted eighth note and one sixteenth note on the end.

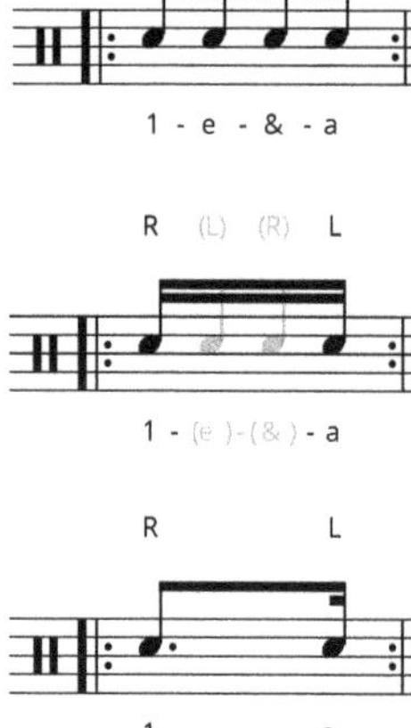

Try to play the figure in sequence on each drum of your drum set.

In the next exercise you play the base figure on each beat in the first bar and the new figure on each beat in the second bar.

FILL VARIATIONS

GROOVES AND FILLS

Tempo

45 65 100

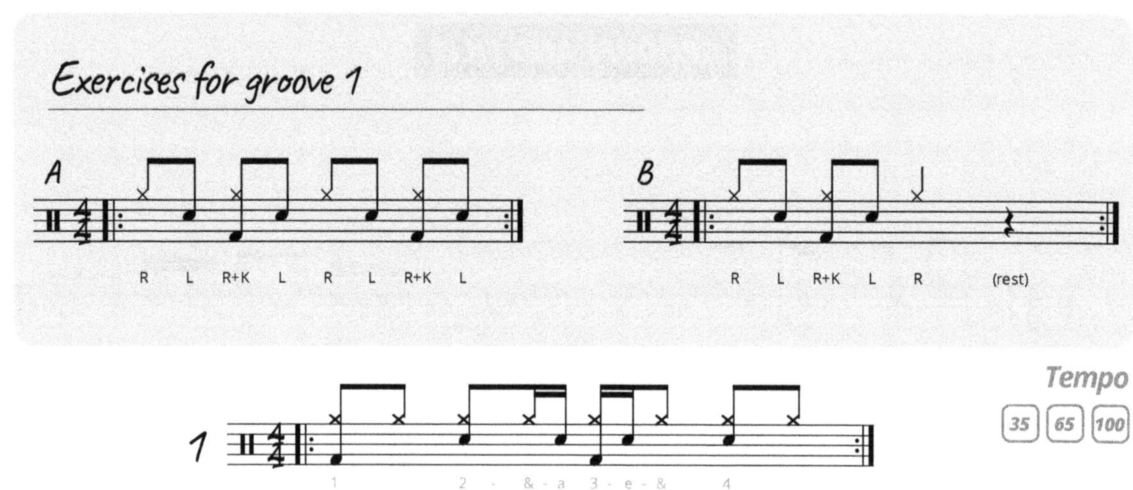
Exercises for groove 1
A
R L R+K L R L R+K L
B
R L R+K L R (rest)
Tempo
35 65 100
1
1 2 - & - a 3 - e - & 4

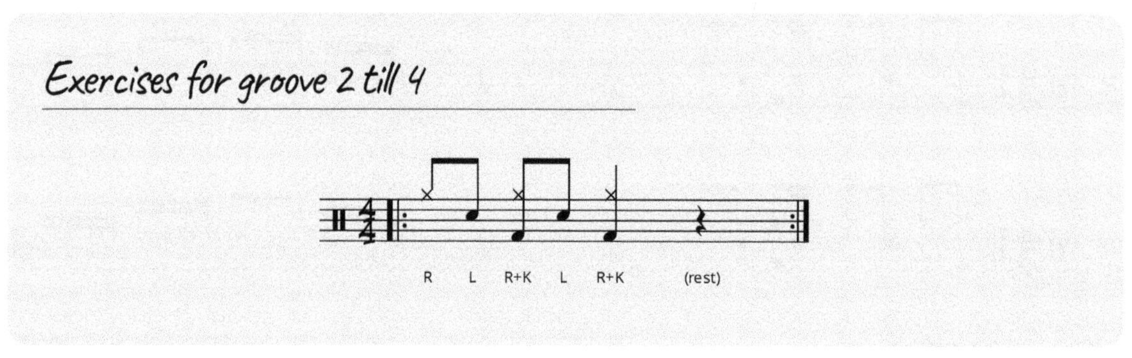
Exercises for groove 2 till 4
R L R+K L R+K (rest)

2
1 2 - & - a 3 - e - & 4
3
1 2 - & - a 3 - e - & 4
4
1 2 - & - a 3 - e - & 4
5
1 2 - & - a 3 - e - & 4
6
1 2 - & - a 3 - e - & 4
7
1 2 - & - a 3 - e - & 4

32 - FILLS - "1 e" fills

We are going to learn a new rhythmical figure. Play the exercises on the snare. Try to say the new figure out loud while you play it.

We start with the base figure that is made out of four sixteenths.

R L R L

1 - e - & - a

We now remove the third and fourth sixteenth note. These are marked with grey and are written in brackets. Play these notes in the air or on the edge of the first tom. Now you hear on the snare what the new figure sounds like.

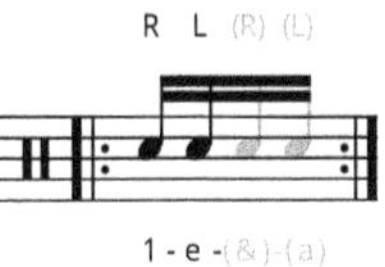

The rhythmical figure is written as followed: one sixteenth note and one dotted eighth note on the end.

Try to play the figure in sequence on each drum of your drum set.

In the next exercise you play the base figure on each beat in the first bar and the new figure on each beat in the second bar.

FILL VARIATIONS

GROOVES AND FILLS

Tempo

45 65 100

33 - GROOVES - *Syncopated kick drum #1*

Now you are going to add sixteenth notes to the groove with the kick drum. You play these kick drum notes exactly in between the strokes of the hi-hat.

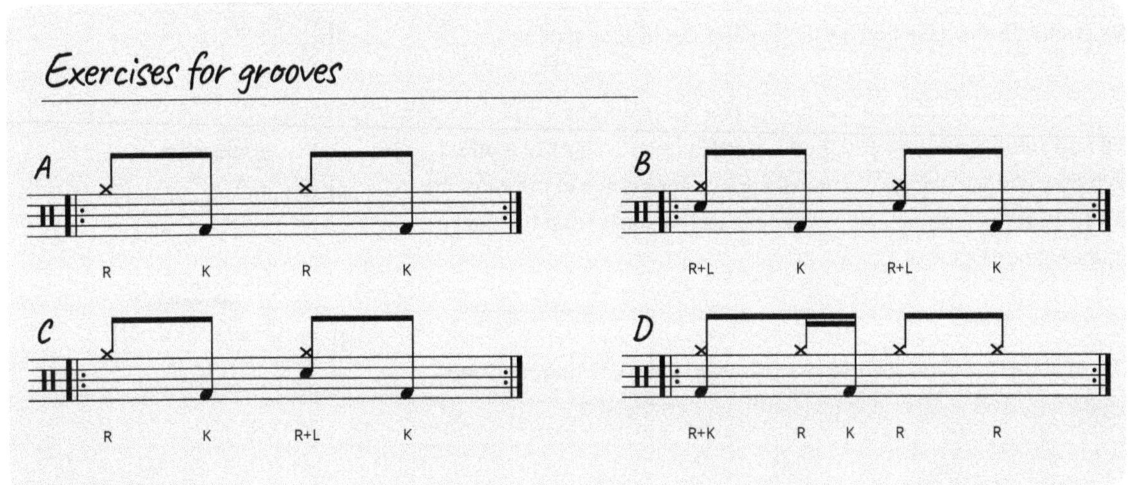

Tempo

34 - FILLS - *"(1) e - a" fills*

We are going to learn a new rhythmical figure. Play the exercises on the snare.
Try to say the new figure out loud while you play it.

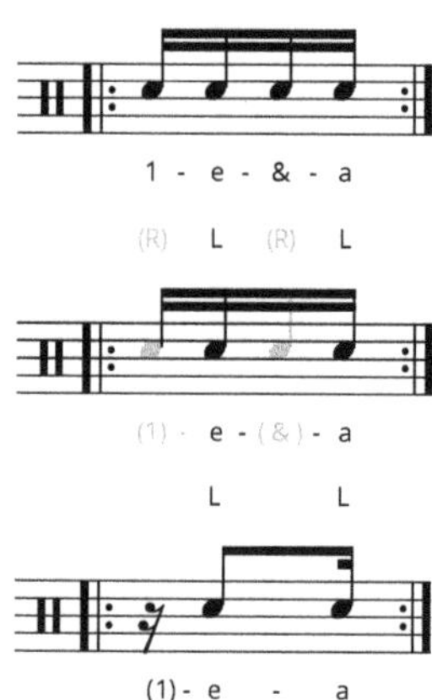

We start with the base figure that is made out of four sixteenths.

We now remove the first and third sixteenth note. These are marked with grey and are written in brackets. Play these notes in the air or on the edge of the first tom. Now you hear on the snare what the new figure sounds like.

The rhythmical figure is written as followed: one sixteenth rest, one eighth note and another one sixteenth note on the end.

Try to play the figure in sequence on each drum of your drum set.

In the next exercise you play the base figure on each beat in the first bar and the new figure on each beat in the second bar.

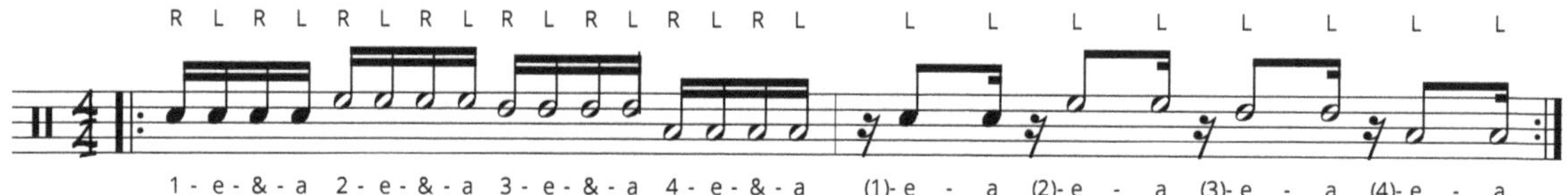

FILL VARIATIONS

GROOVES AND FILLS

Tempo

45 65 100

35 - GROOVES - *Syncopated kick drum #2*

Tempo

36 - GROOVES - *2 bar quarter note hi-hat grooves*

The next grooves are divided over the two bars. The hi-hat is played in quarters.
Try to play the groove from memory after you have repeated it a couple of times first.

Tempo

70 100 130

37 - FILLS - *Adding a kick drum (RLRK)*

You will now add kick drums to your fills.

Tempo

45 65 100

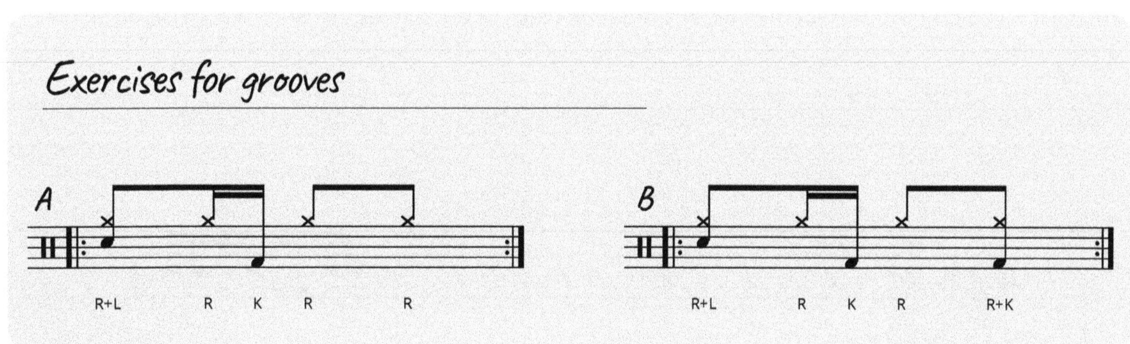
Exercises for grooves
A
R+L
R
K
R
R
B
R+L
R
K
R
R+K

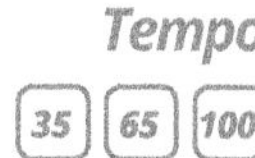
Tempo
35
65
100

1
1 2 - & - a (3) - & 4
2
1 - & 2 - & - a (3) - & 4
3
1 - & - a 2 - & - a (3) - & 4
4
1 - & - a 2 - & - a 3 - e - & 4
5
1 - & - a 2 - & - a 3 - e - & 4 - & - a

39 - FILLS - *Adding two kick drums (RLKK)*

In these fills you play two kick drum notes one after the other. Make sure all the notes are the same length.

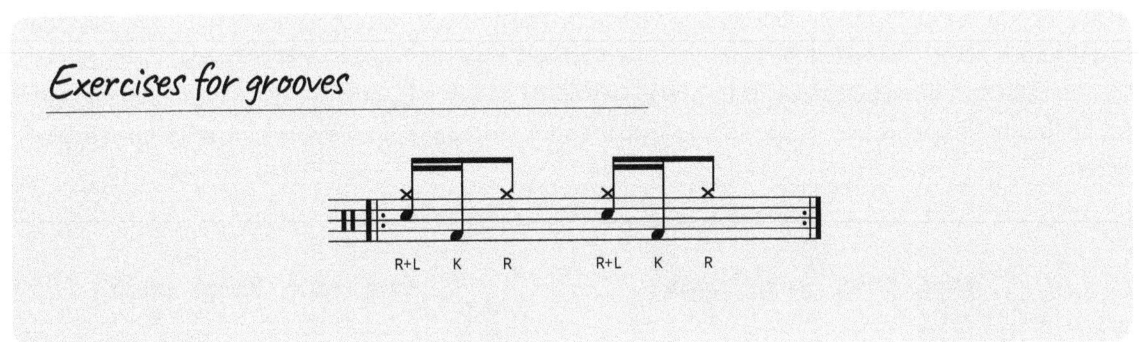

Tempo

35 65 100

41 - FILLS - *Snare accents #1*

An accent is indicated by this symbol (>) above the note. The note with the accent needs to be played louder than the other notes. The rest of the notes in these exercises are written down smaller than you are used to. This indicates that these notes need to be played very softly. These soft notes are also called "ghost notes". You lift the stick higher to play loudly and you keep the stick as low as possible above the drum head to play softer.

Tempo

30 50 90

1

2

3

4

5

6

7

8

9

10

11

12

Practice tips (example fill 10)

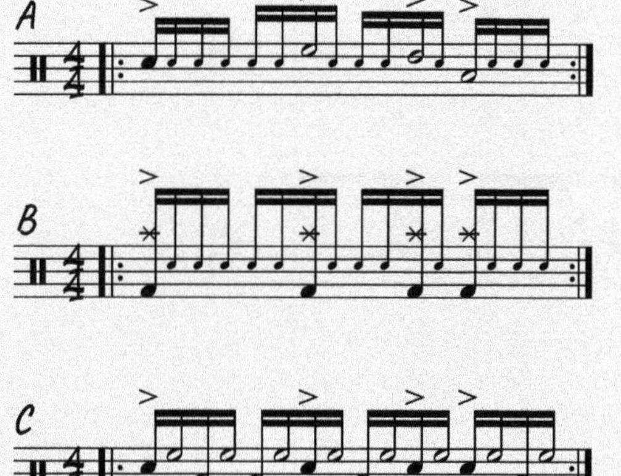

Play the accents on the snare and toms. You keep playing the ghost notes on the snare.

Play the accents on the cymbals or open hi-hat together with the kick drum.

Play the accents on the snare.
Play the other notes with the left hand on the high tom and with the right hand on the floor tom.

Exercises for groove 1 and 2

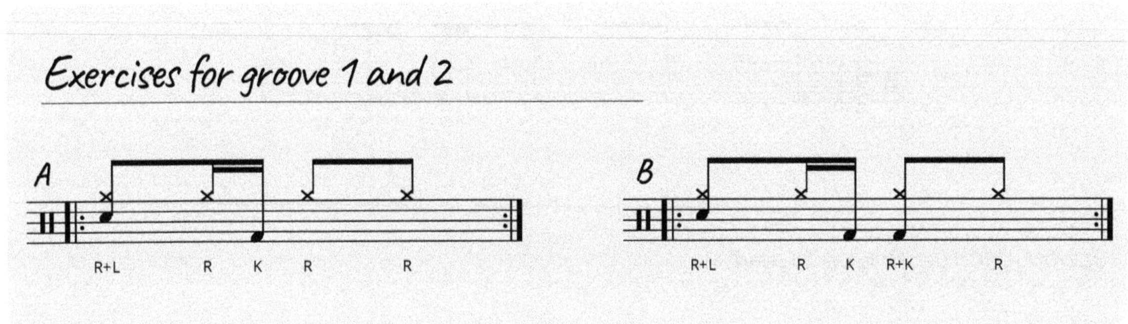

Tempo

Exercises for groove 3

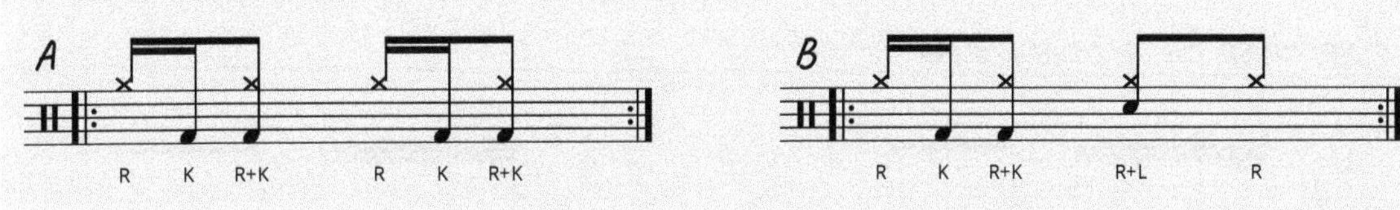

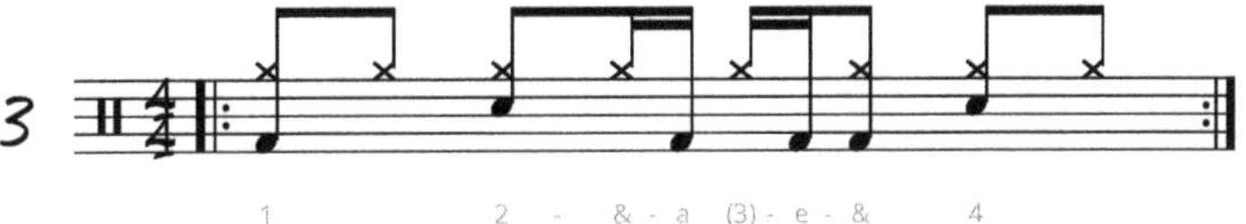

Exercises for groove 4 and 5

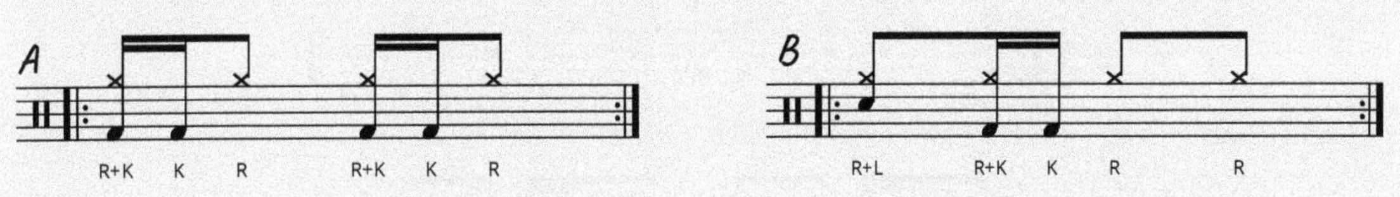

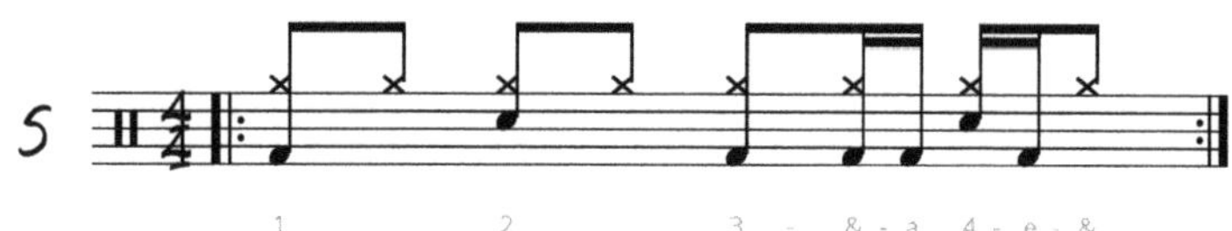
5
1 2 3 - & - a 4 - e - &

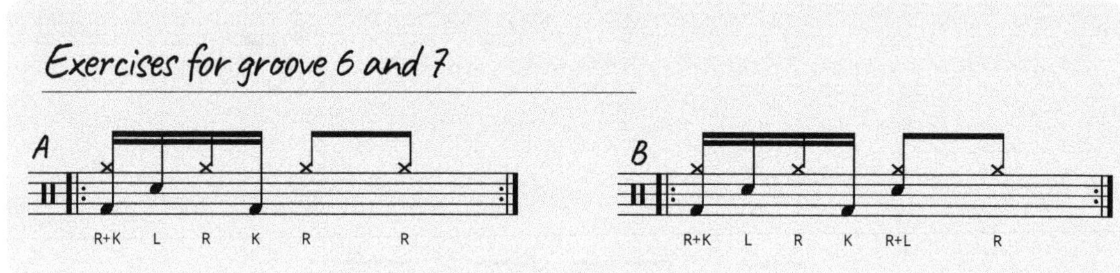
Exercises for groove 6 and 7
A
R+K L R K R R
B
R+K L R K R+L R

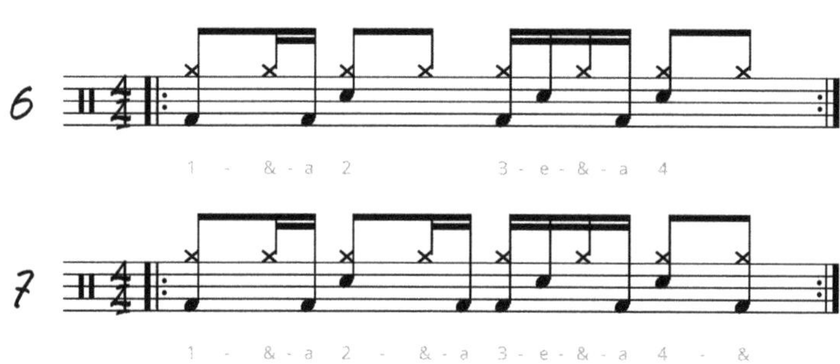
6
1 - & - a 2 3 - e - & - a 4
7
1 - & - a 2 - & - a 3 - e - & - a 4 - &

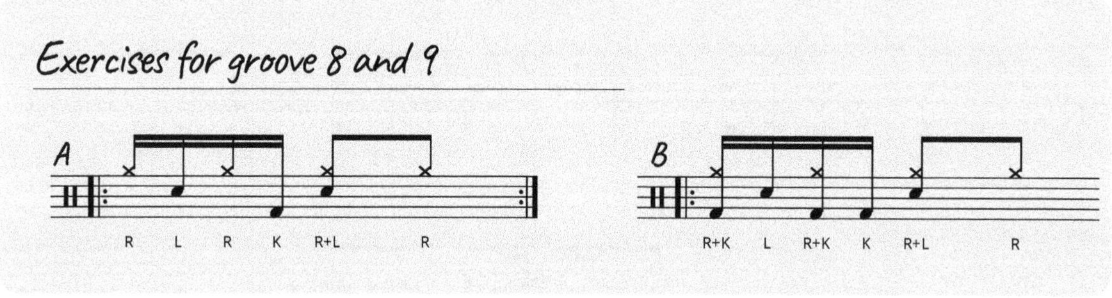
Exercises for groove 8 and 9
A
R L R K R+L R
B
R+K L R+K K R+L R

8
1 - e - & - a 2 - & - 3 4
9
1 - & - a 2 - & - a 3 - e - & - a 4
10
1 - & - a 2 - & 3 - & - a 4 - &

43 - FILLS - *Groovy fills*

We play grooves on the hi-hat or ride, together with the snare and kick drum. These fills are being played on the same parts of the drum set as with the grooves. The hi-hat is played in eighths, but because the kick drum and snare drum patterns change, a fill is created. The pattern can be recognized by the gray outline.

In a 12/8 groove we play three 8th notes in one beat, so twelve in a whole measure. We now count the eights as 1-&-a 2-&-a 3-&-a 4-&-a (pronounce "&-a" as "and-ah"). These grooves and the shuffle grooves (chapter 49) are often used in blues, jazz and rock 'n' roll songs.

Exercises for groove 1

A

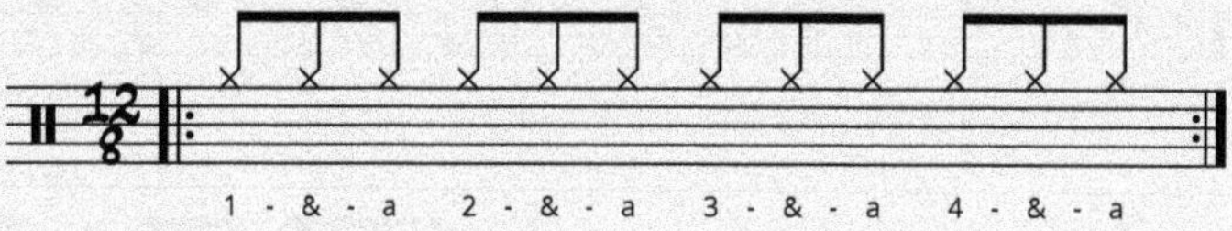

1 - & - a 2 - & - a 3 - & - a 4 - & - a

B

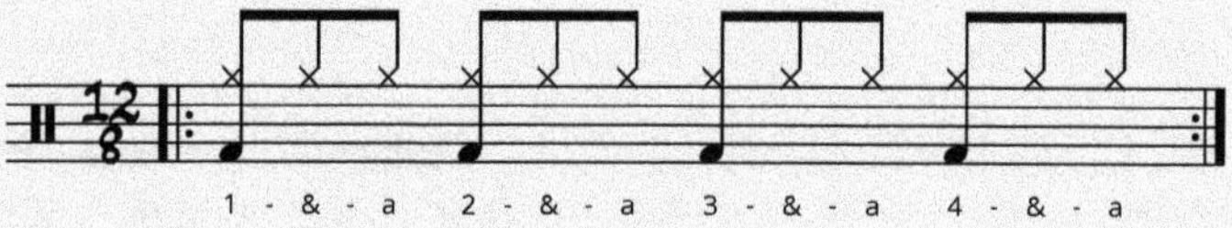

1 - & - a 2 - & - a 3 - & - a 4 - & - a

C

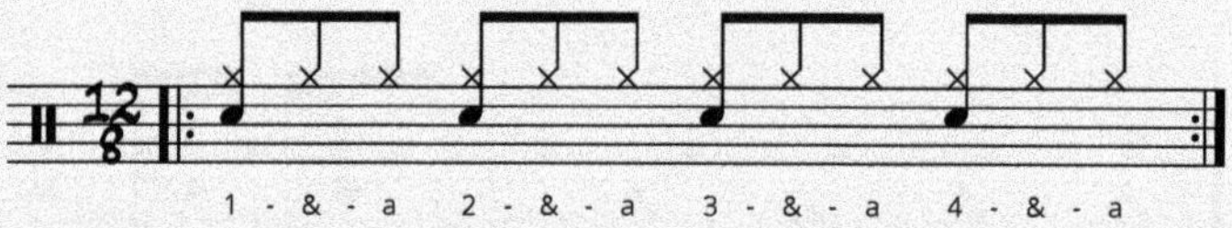

1 - & - a 2 - & - a 3 - & - a 4 - & - a

D

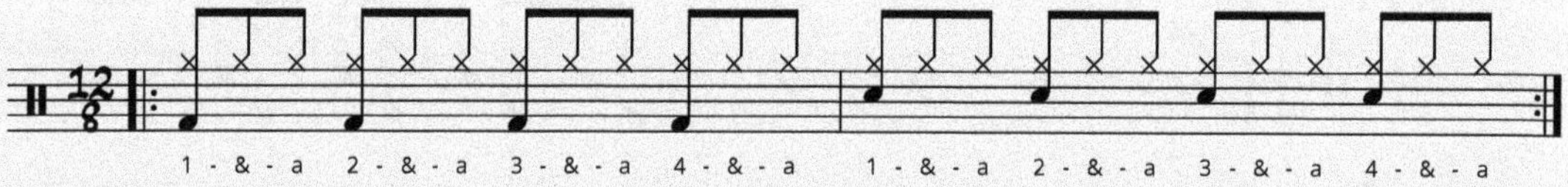

1 - & - a 2 - & - a 3 - & - a 4 - & - a 1 - & - a 2 - & - a 3 - & - a 4 - & - a

E

1 - & - a 2 - & - a 3 - & - a 4 - & - a

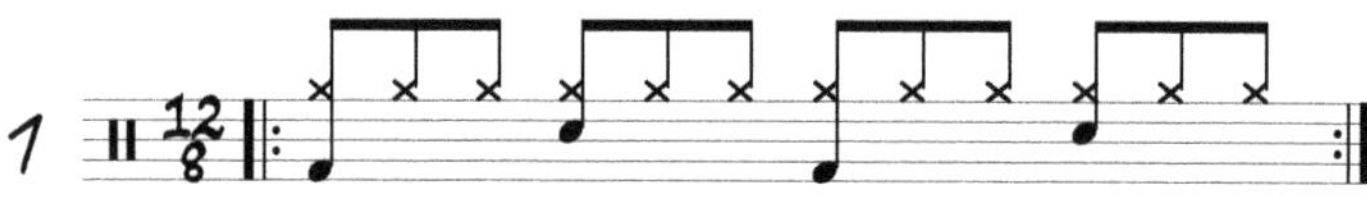

Exercises for groove 2 and 3

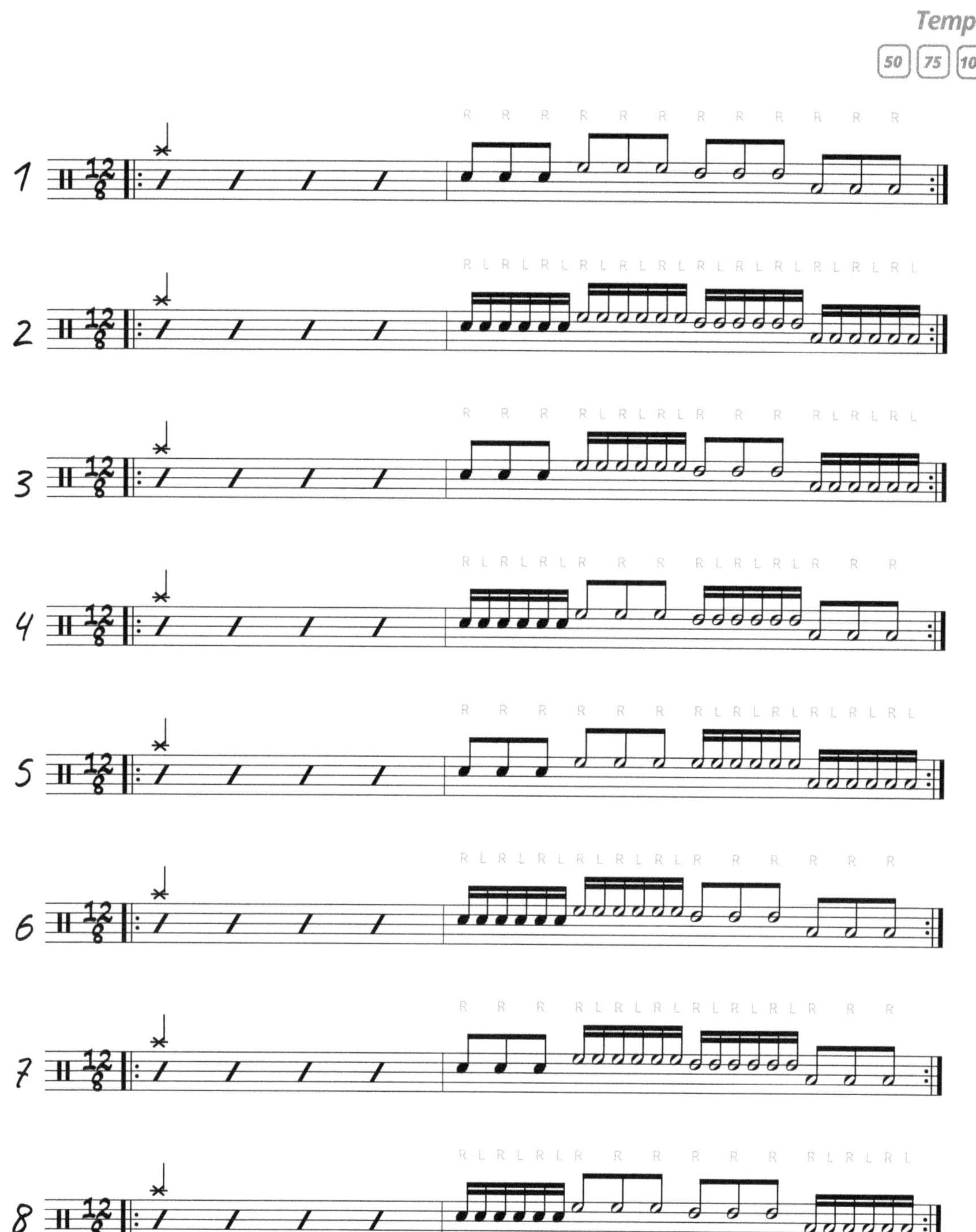
Tempo
50
75
100
1
R R R R R R R R R R R R
2
R L R L R L R L R L R L R L R L R L R L R L R L
3
R R R R L R L R L R R R L R L R L
4
R L R L R L R R R R L R L R L R R R
5
R R R R R R R L R L R L R L R L R L
6
R L R L R L R L R L R L R R R R R R
7
R R R R L R L R L R L R L R L R R R
8
R L R L R L R R R R R R R L R L R L

46 - GROOVES - *Twelve-eight grooves #2*

You will now add sixteenth notes to the groove with the kick drum and snare drum. You play these notes exactly in between the strokes of the hi-hat.

Tempo

50 75 100

Tempo

50 75 100

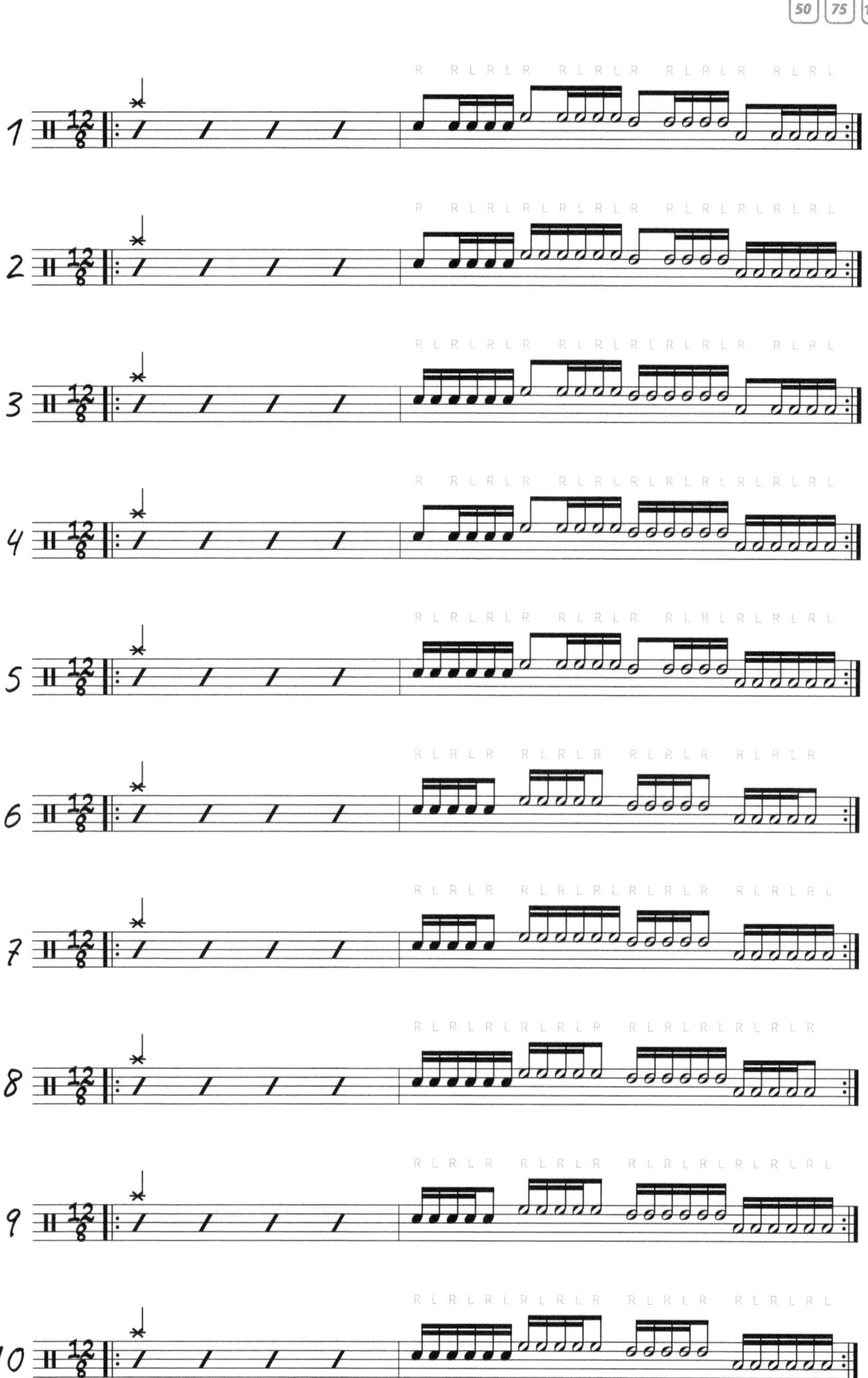

48 - FILLS - *Twelve-eight fills #3*

Tempo

50 75 100

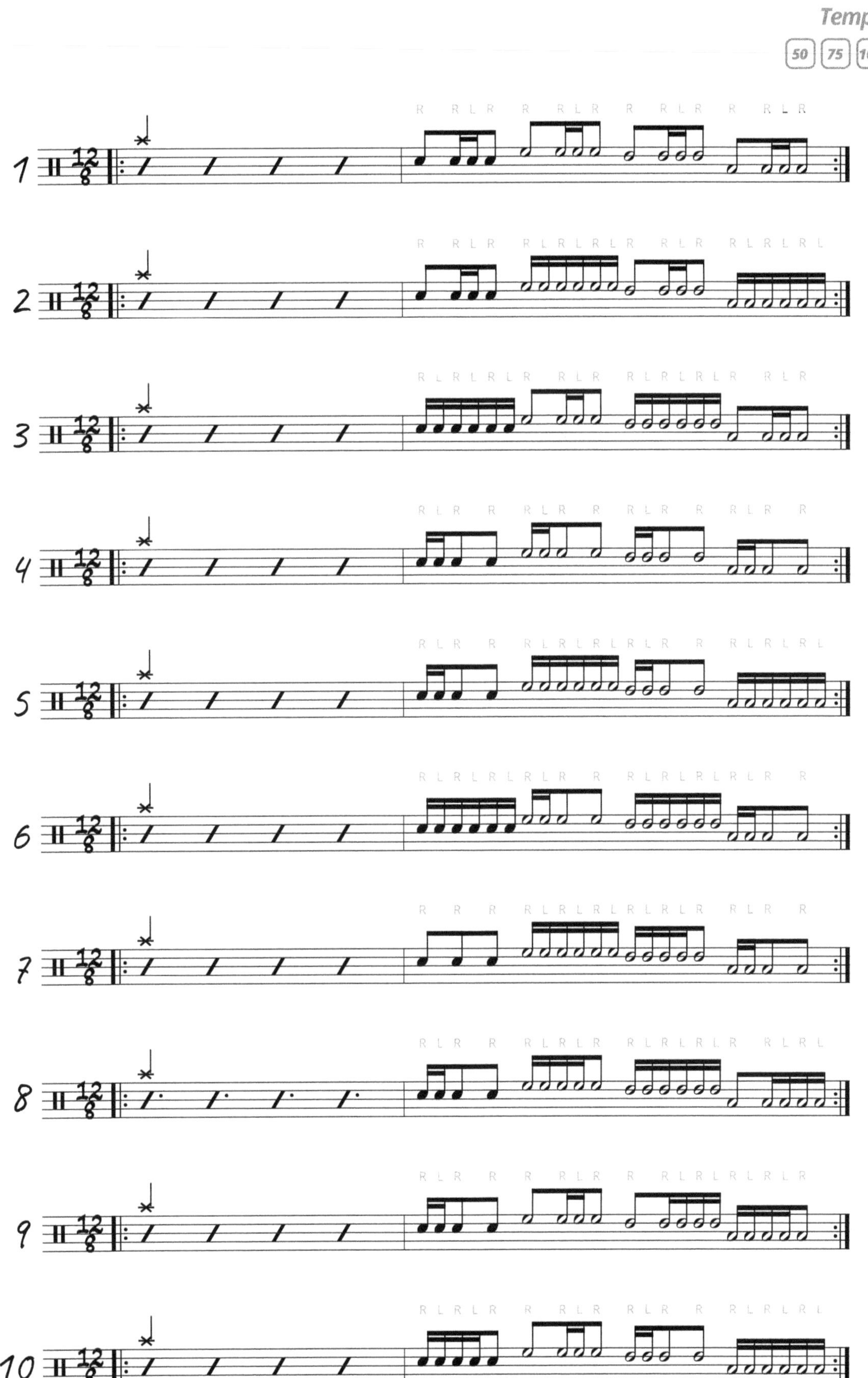

49 - GROOVES - *Shuffle grooves*

Shuffle grooves are derived from the 12/8 grooves. They both have three strokes per beat and are also called grooves with a triplet or swing feel. The hi-hat pattern in the beat is a characteristic of the shuffle. The beat consists of one stroke followed by a rest and then another stroke. These grooves are faster to play the 12/8 grooves because of the rest in between the two notes. The shuffle grooves are written down as triplets in a 4/4-time signature. That is why there is a small 3 above the beat.

Exercises for groove 1

A
3 3 3 3
1 - (&) - a 2 - (&) - a 3 - (&) - a 4 - (&) - a

B
3 3 3 3
1 - (&) - a 2 - (&) - a 3 - (&) - a 4 - (&) - a

C
3 3 3 3
1 - (&) - a 2 - (&) - a 3 - (&) - a 4 - (&) - a

D
3 3 3 3 3 3 3 3
1 - (&) - a 2 - (&) - a 3 - (&) - a 4 - (&) - a 1 - (&) - a 2 - (&) - a 3 - (&) - a 4 - (&) - a

E
3 3 3 3
1 - (&) - a 2 - (n&) - a 3 - (&) - a 4 - (&) - a

Tempo

70 100 140

1
3 3 3 3

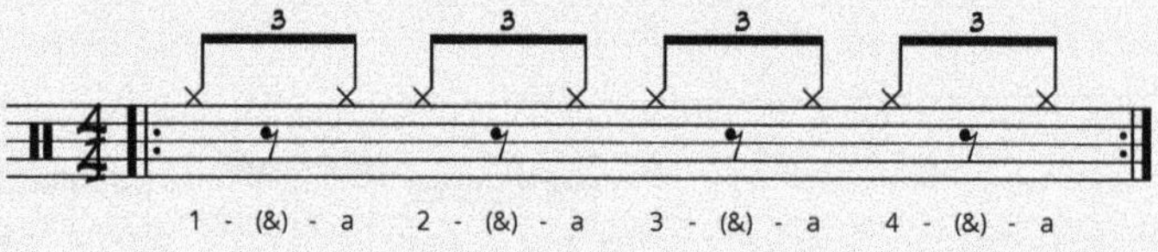

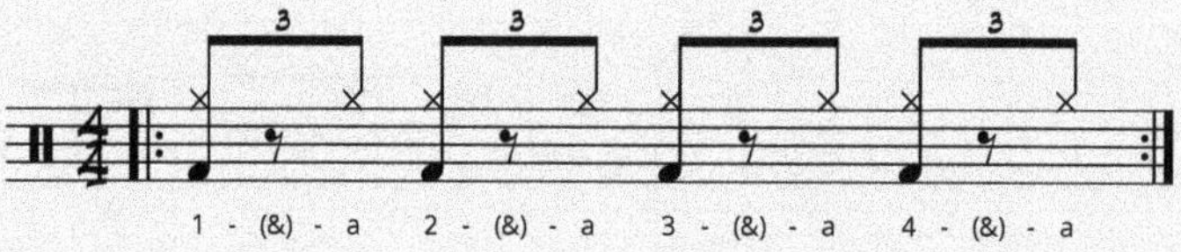

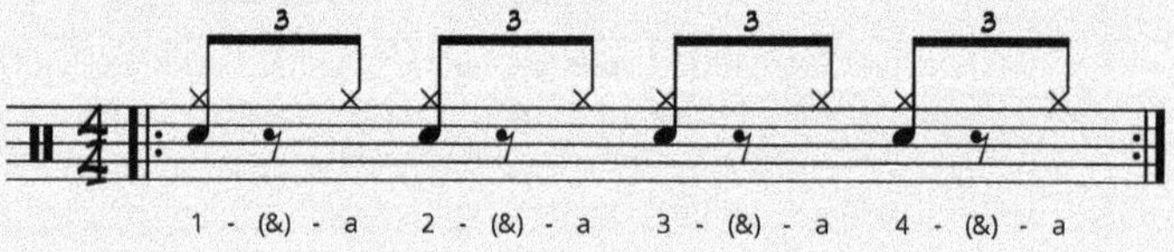

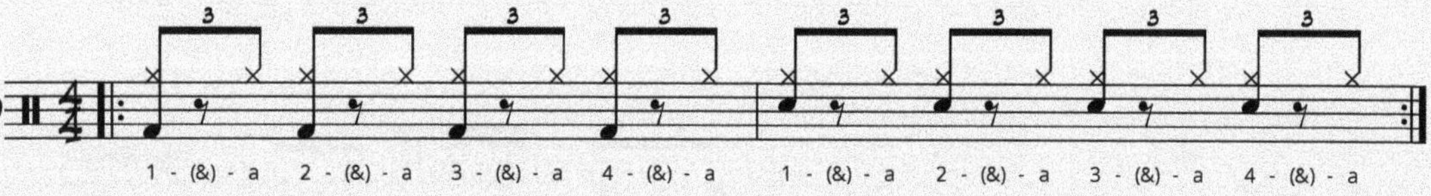

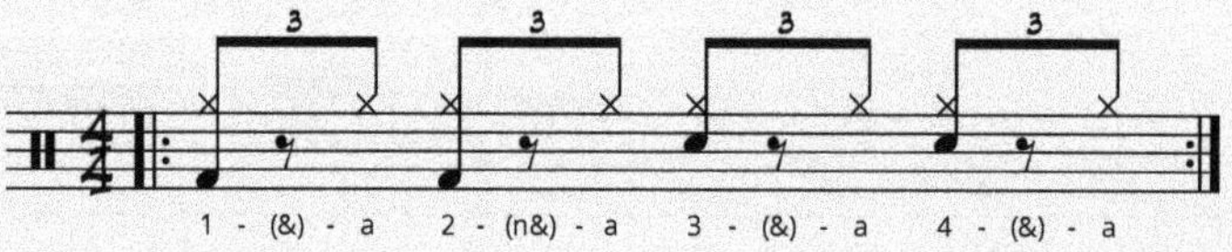

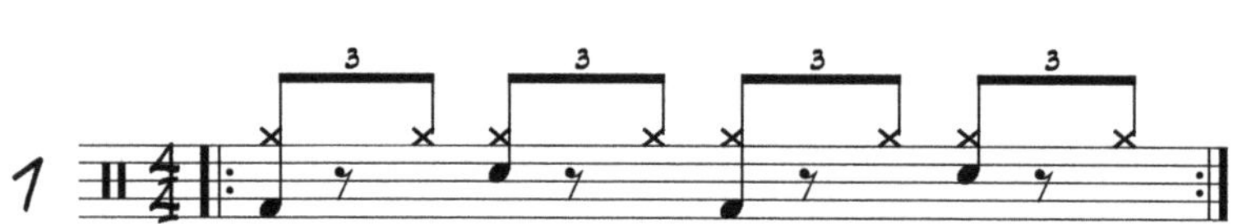

Exercises for groove 2

1 - (&) - a 2 - (&) - a 3 - (&) - a 4 - (&) - a

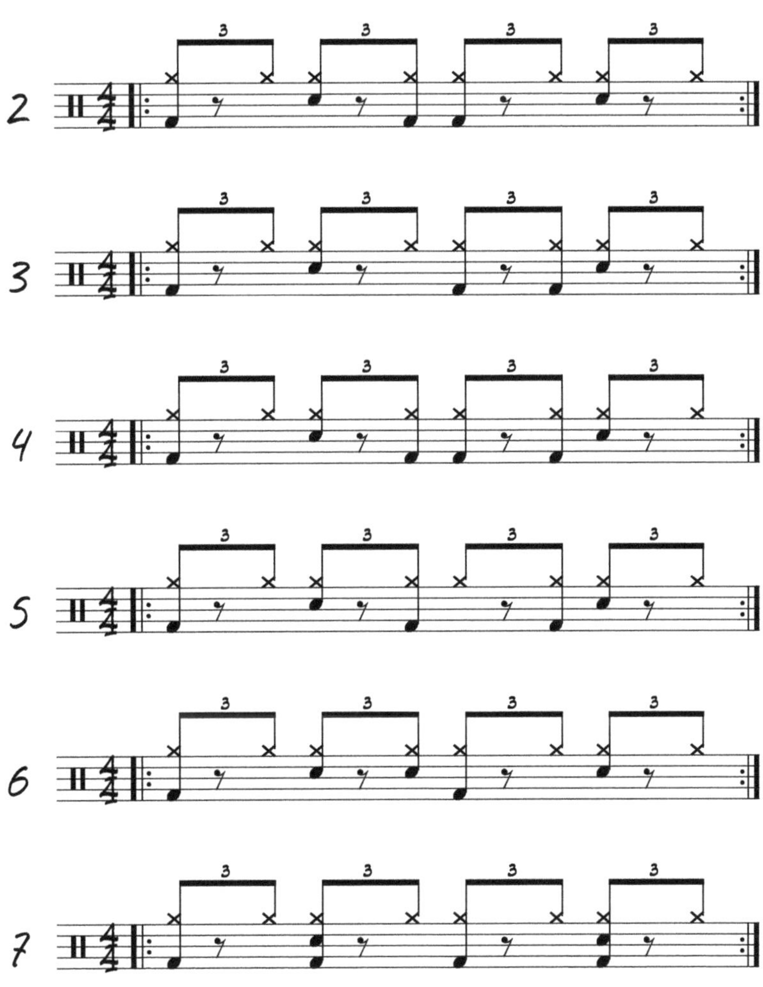

Tempo
70 100 140

51 - GROOVES - *Sixteenth note hi-hat (RLRL) #2*

Tempo

25 65 95

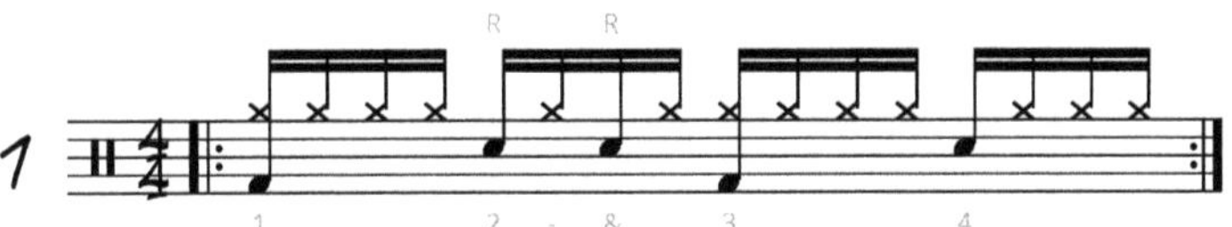

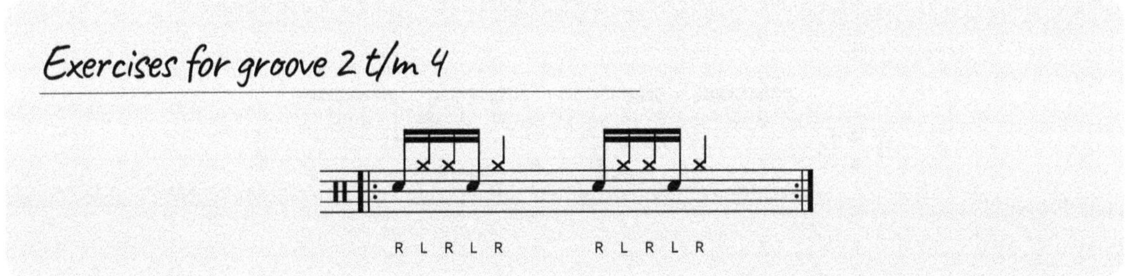

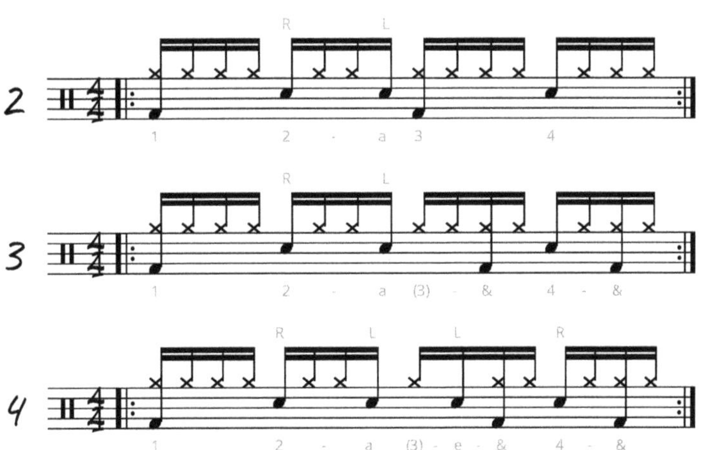

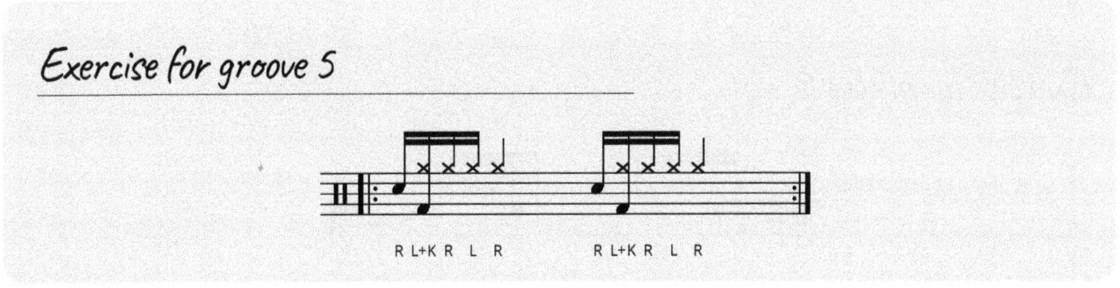

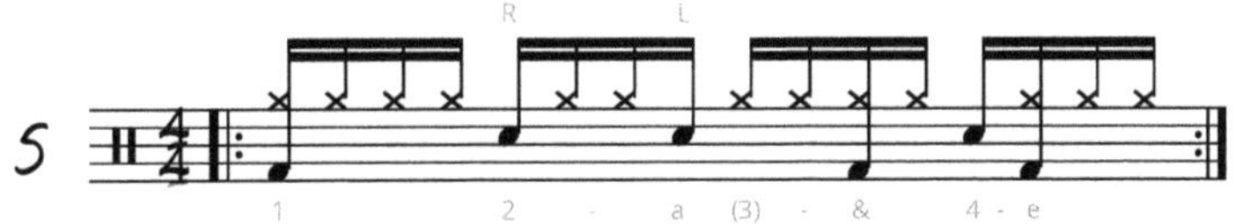

51 - GROOVES - *Sixteenth note hi-hat (RLRL) #2*

Exercise for groove 6

R+K L R L+K R R+K L R L+K R

Exercises for groove 7 and 8

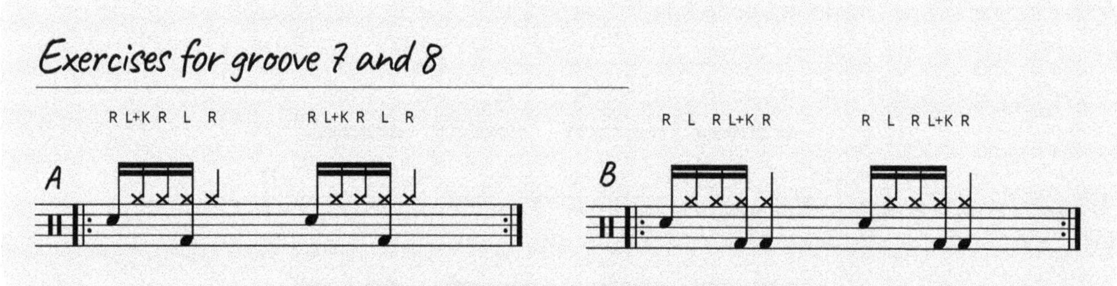

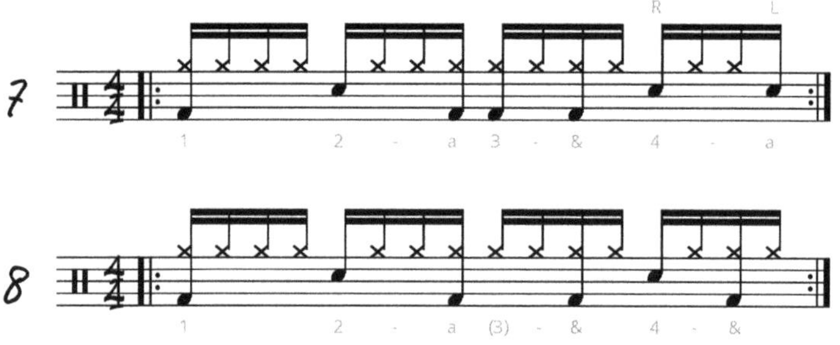

Exercise for groove 9

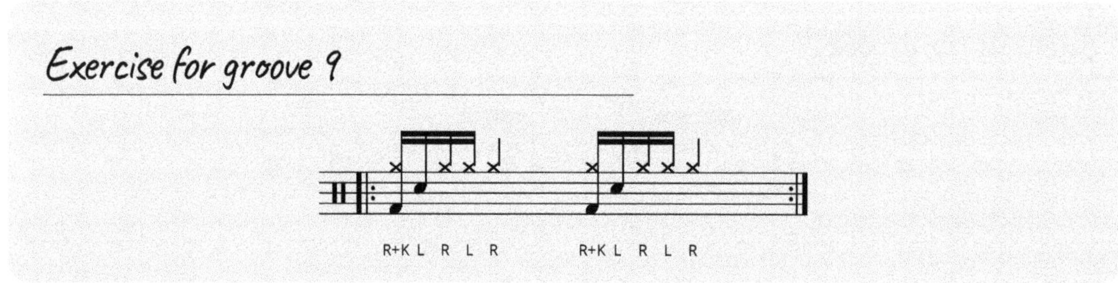

52 - FILLS - *Snare accents #2*

You will now play accents with both your right hand and your left hand.
Exercises 11 and 12 are also called "train beats".

Tempo

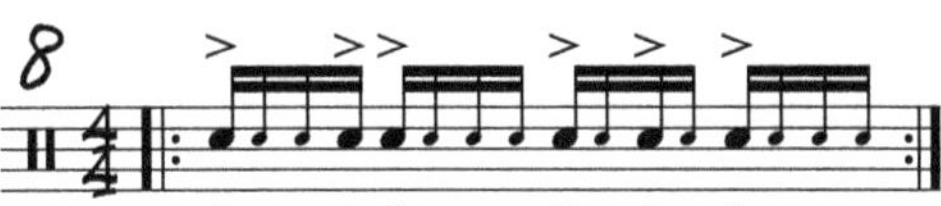

Practice tips (example fill 3)

Play the accents on the snare and toms. You keep playing the ghost notes on the snare.

Play the accents on the cymbals or open hi-hat together with the kick drum.

Play the accents on the snare.
Play the other notes with the left hand on the high tom and with the right hand on the floor tom.

Play the patterns D, E and F with your feet during the exercises.

53 - GROOVES - *Sixteenth note hi-hat (RRRR) #2*

Tempo

30 50 75

54 - TECHNIQUE - *Paradiddle*

The paradiddle consists of single and double strokes and is one of the most important rudiments:

Always keep practicing the paradiddle at speed. You will now use the paradiddle to make grooves and fills.

GROOVES

Tempo
45 65 100

1
R L R R L R L L

2
R L R R L R L L R L R R L R L L

3
R L R R L R L L R L R R L R L L

4
R L R R L R L L R L R R L R L L

FILLS

By placing accents in the paradiddle, you create a different rhythm each time. You can then place the accents on different parts of the drum set. You can keep playing the ghost notes on the snare.
Two fills are shown each time based on new accents in the paradiddle.
Try to think of some fills yourself this way.

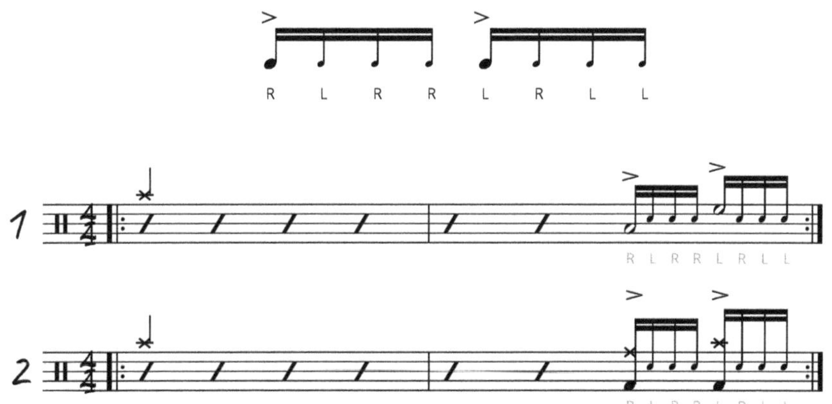

R L R R L R L L
3
R L R R L R L L
4
R L R R L R L L
R L R R L R L L
5
R L R R L R L L
6
R L R R L R L L
R L R R L R L L
7
R L R R L R L L
8
R L R R L R L L
R L R R L R L L
9
R L R R L R L L
10
R L R R L R L L

55 - GROOVES - *Crash accents #2*

Tempo

45 70 90

Accents can be played in combination with fills.
The accents are the same as in exercise 1, 2 and 4, but are now introduced with fills.

You can also divide the strokes of the fills over the toms.
This is the same fill as in exercise 6, but in combination with the toms.

56 - TECHNIQUE - *Single stroke four*

The single stroke four is a rhythmical figure with a triplet worked into it and is officially played alternately (RLRL or LRLR). In these grooves and fills you will also use different hand positions and make combinations with the kick drum.

GROOVES

Exercises for groove fill 3 till 6

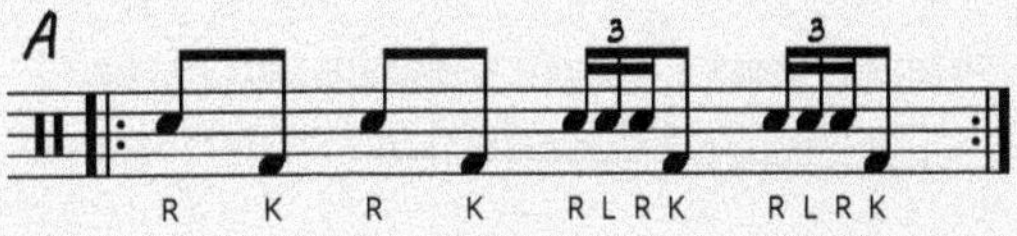
A
3 3
R K R K RLRK RLRK

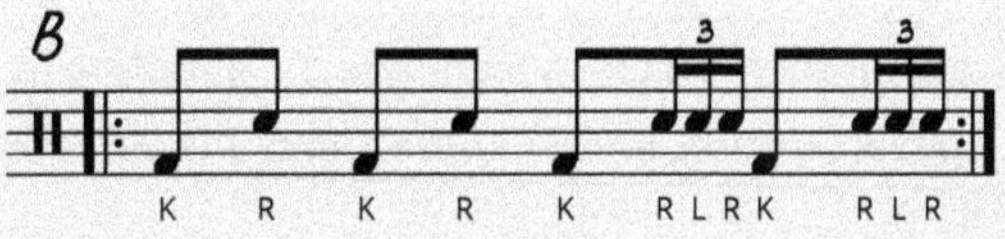
B
3 3
K R K R K RLRK RLR

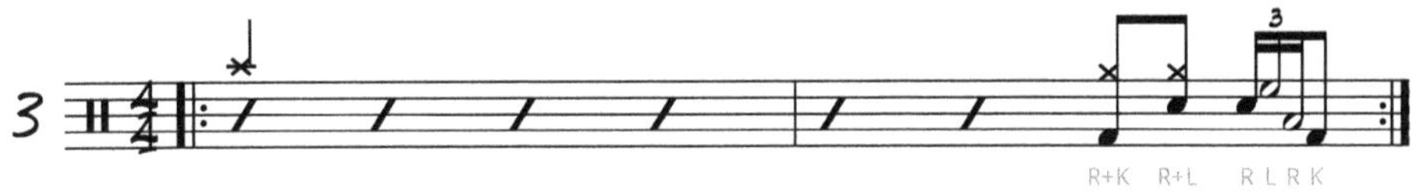
3
R+K R+L RLRK

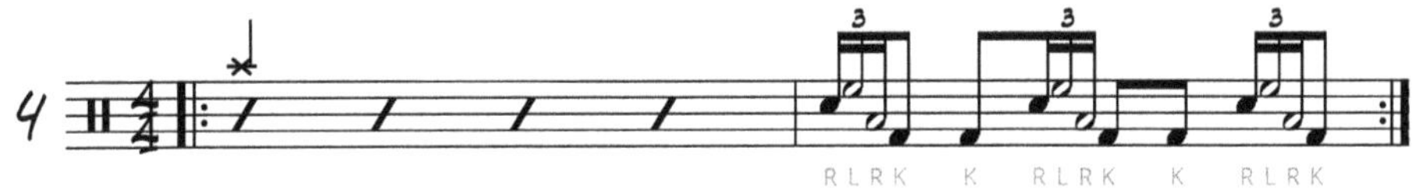
4
RLRK K RLRK K RLRK

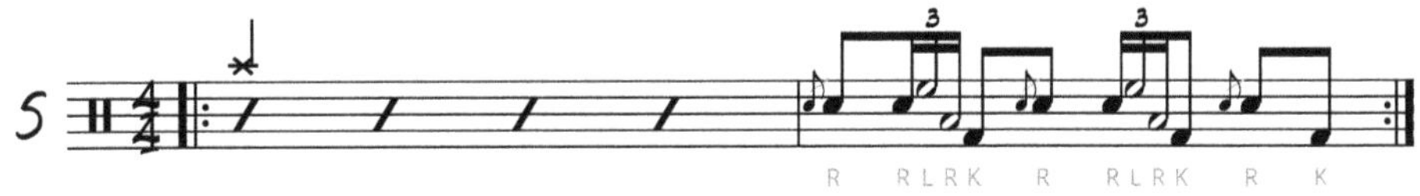
5
R RLRK R RLRK R K

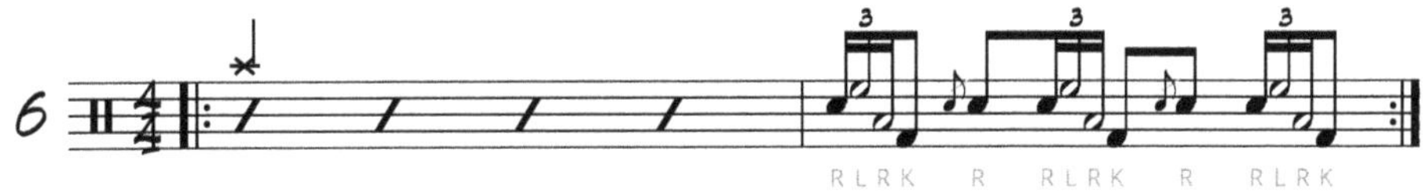
6
RLRK R RLRK R RLRK

Exercises for fill 7 till 10

K R K R KRLR KRLR

7
KRLR KRLR KRLR R L R

8
KRLR RLRK

9
KRLR R KRLR R KRLR

10
KRLR L R L KRLR L R L KRLR L

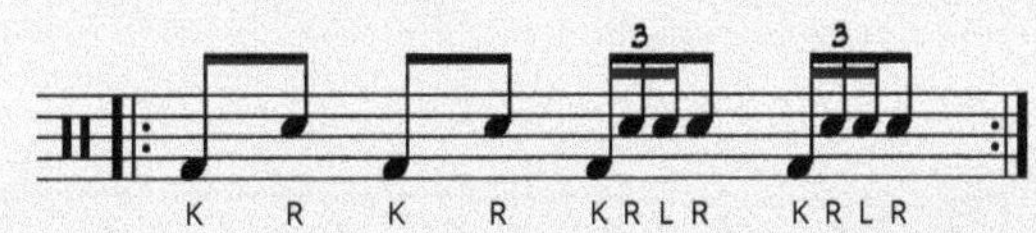

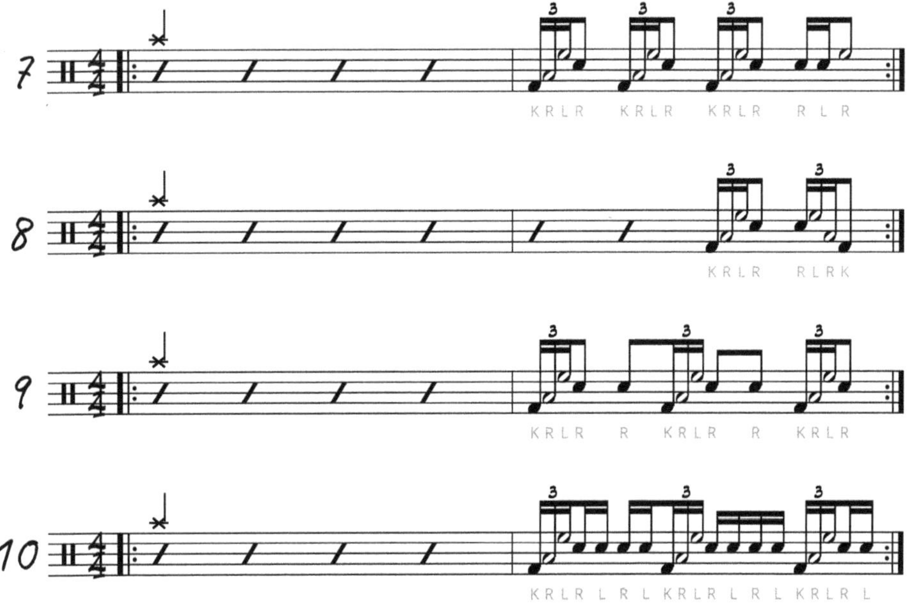

57 - FILLS & GROOVES - Song structure

Songs are divided into parts, like an intro, verse, chorus and bridge. We call the order of these parts the structure of the song. An example of a common structure is: intro – verse – chorus – verse – chorus – bridge – chorus – chorus – outro.

As a drummer you can accentuate the structure by playing a different groove in each separate part of the song (verse, chorus, etc.) At the end of the part you can play a fill to introduce the transition to a different part.

The parts of a song (verse, chorus etc.) usually consist of multiple lines of 4, 8 or 16 measures. You can then also accentuate these lines by finishing them with a short fill in the last measure.

Practice this concept with the next scheme. This scheme could for example be a verse. You can see fills of different lengths are being played. The slash lines indicate the four beats in the measure. The idea is to play the groove in this measure.

Try repeating the scheme as many times until you can feel which measure you are in and you don't need to count anymore. It helps to sing a random melody or chorus. Listen well to see which tone or word the fill should start on.

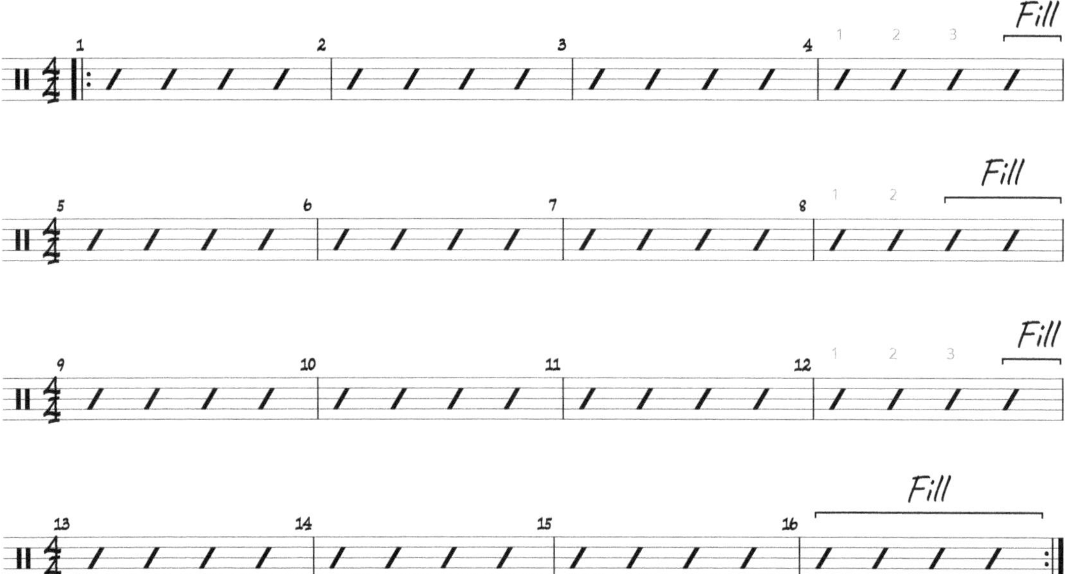

58 - TECHNIQUE - *Inverted paradiddle*

A variation on the paradiddle is the inverted paradiddle. This one again consists of single and double strokes.

Also keep practicing this inverted paradiddle at speed.
You will now use the inverted paradiddle to make grooves and fills.

Tempo
45 65 100

The inverted paradiddle followed by the normal paradiddle:

FILLS

By placing accents in the inverted paradiddle, you create a different rhythm each time. You can then place the accents on different parts of the drum set. You can keep playing the ghost notes on the snare.
Two fills are shown each time based on new accents in the paradiddle.
Try to think of some fills yourself this way.

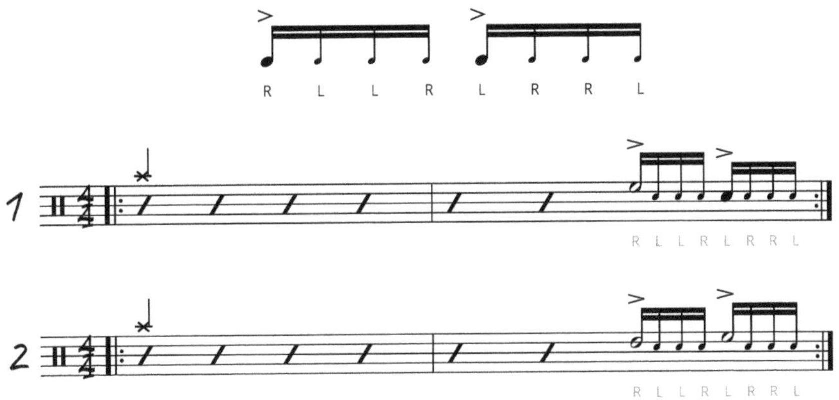

58 - TECHNIQUE - *Inverted paradiddle*

We will use creative ways to change the grooves you have learned. You can apply these ways to each groove in this book. Like this you will be able to create an unending number of new grooves.

We use two grooves as an example in this chapter and we show which creative ways you can apply to changes these grooves.

HI-HAT VARIATIONS

In the examples the hi-hat is played in eighths. Try to play the following hi-hat patterns.
The kick drum and snare drum notes remain unchanged.

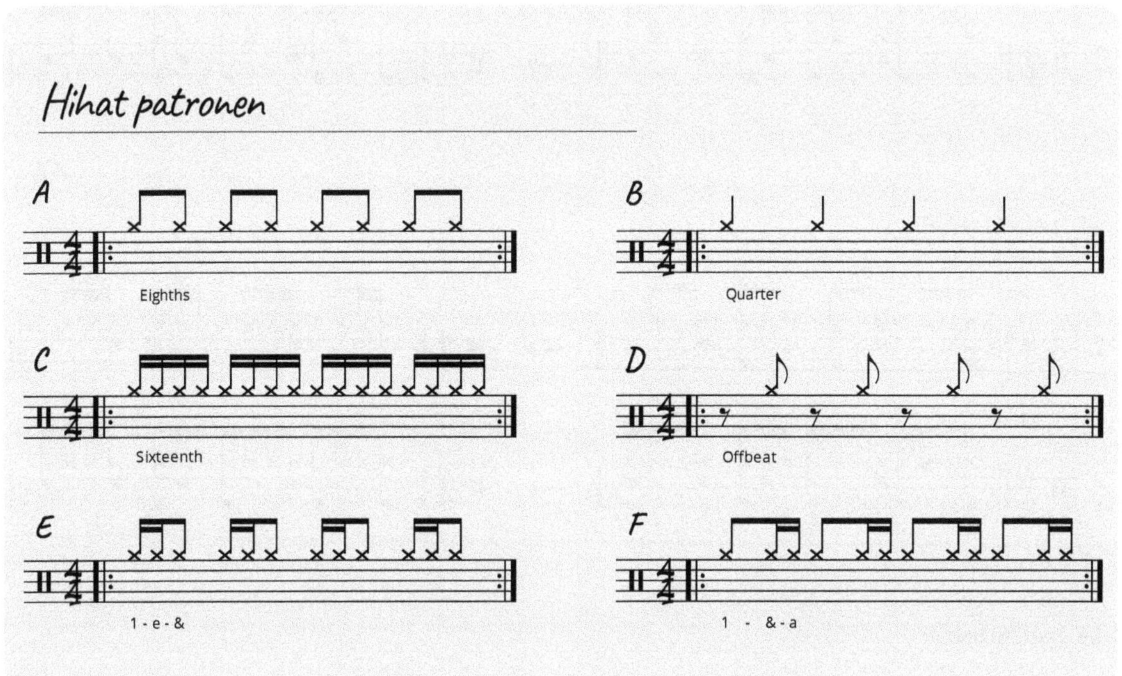

The examples will look as followed:

Quarter note hi-hat:

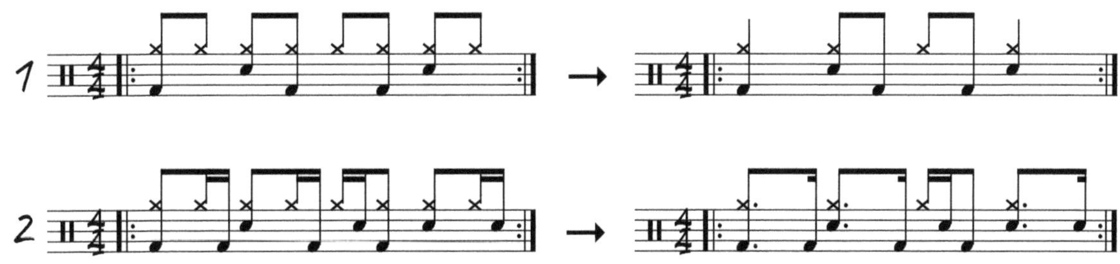

Sixteenth note hi-hat::

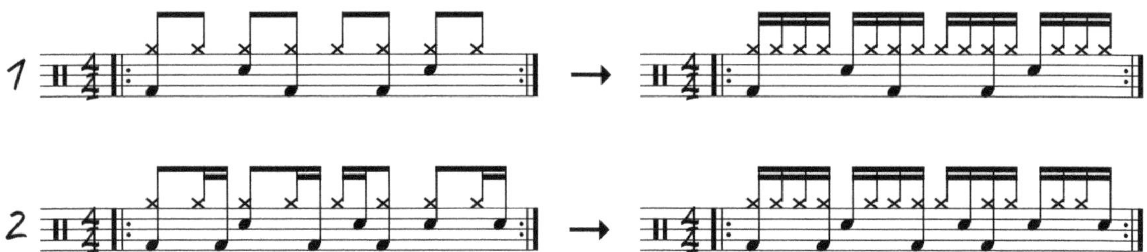

Offbeat hi-hat::

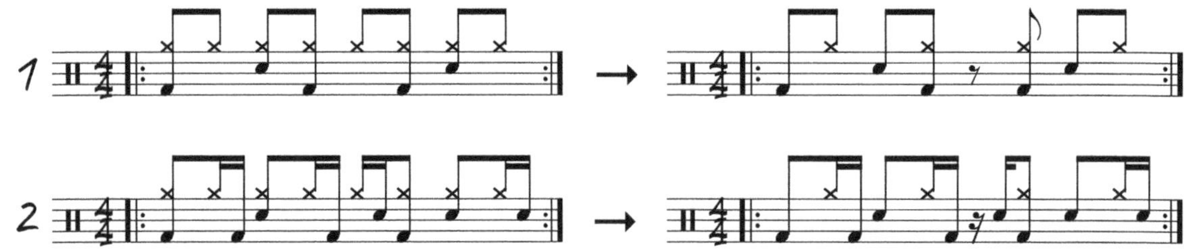

"1-e-&" pattern hi-hat:

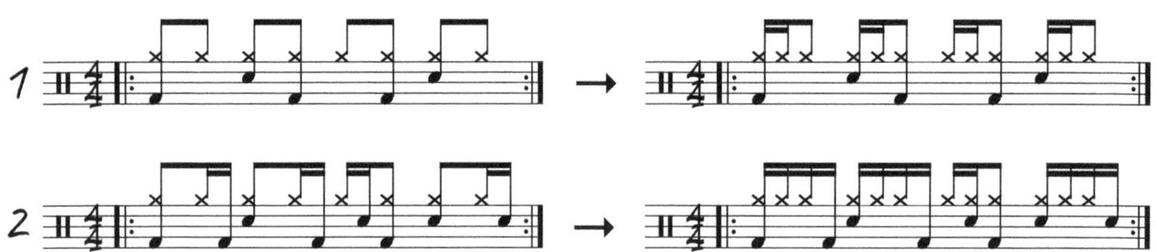

"1-&a" pattern hi-hat:

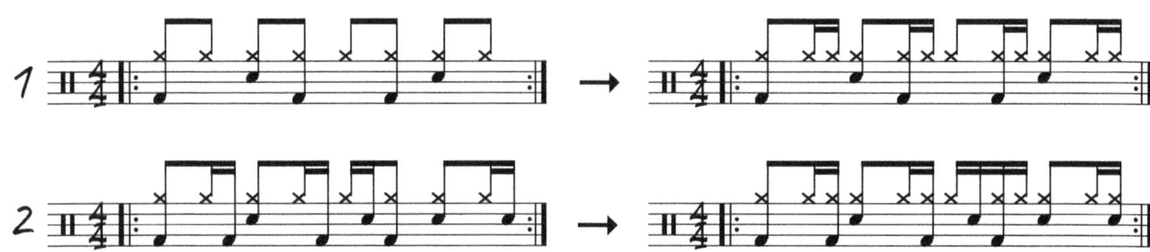

SPLITTING HANDS

We can further extend the groove variation with the hi-hat in sixteenths by playing the hi-hat pattern on different parts of the drum set. Play the right hand on the ride and the left hand on the hi-hat.

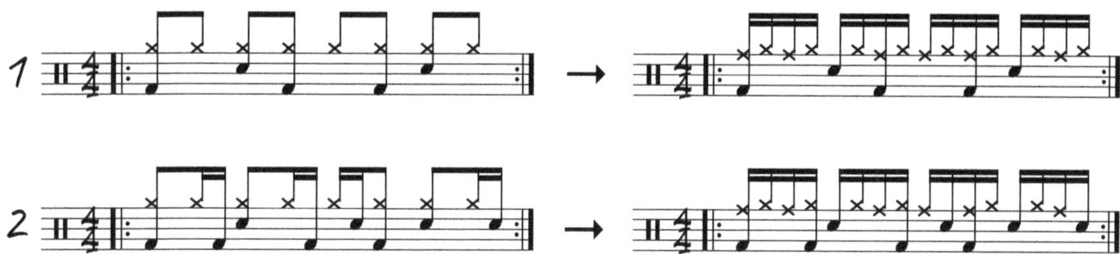

You can also move the left hand to the snare. Now play the notes you would normally play with left on the hi-hat as soft ghost notes on the snare.

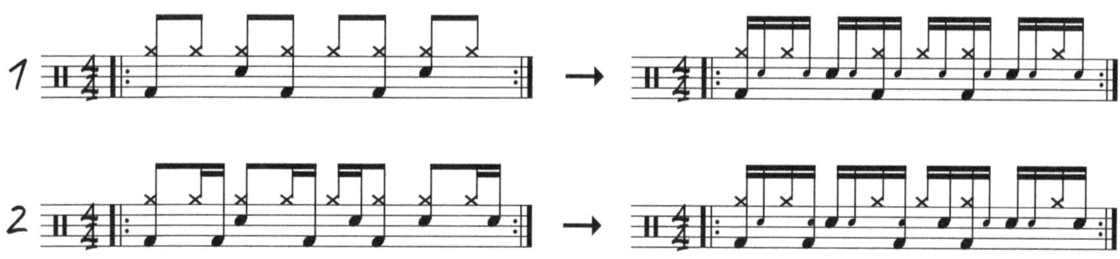

HIHAT ACCENTS

Try playing accents on the hi-hat with your right hand. Play the notes with accents louder than the other notes. This way the groove sounds firm and tight.

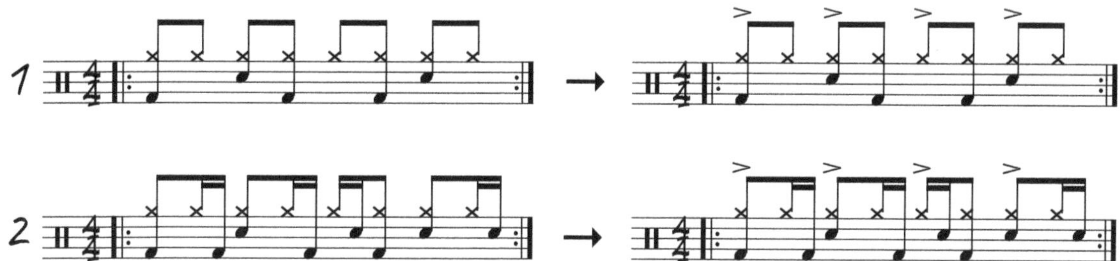

ADDING OPEN HI-HAT

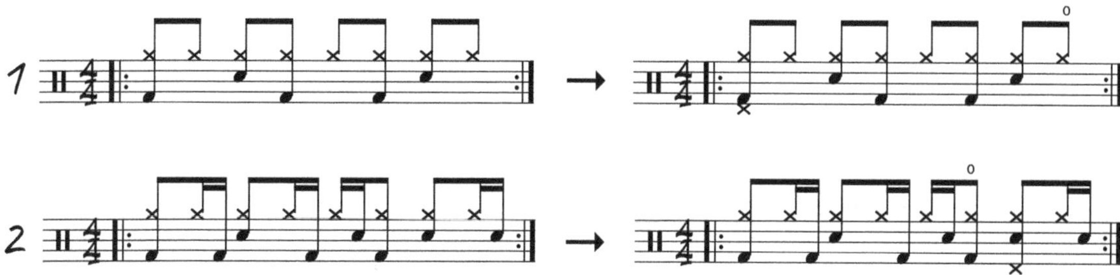

ADDING SNARE DRUM OR KICK DRUM

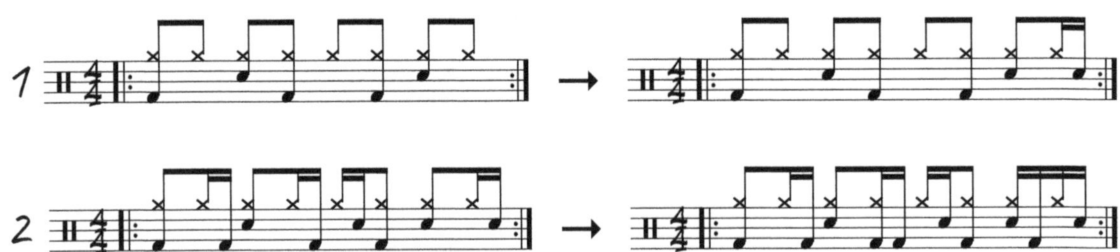

LEAVING OUT BACK BEAT

Back beats are the snare drum notes on the second and fourth beat. In these examples you leave out the first back beat. This gives the groove more space and an open character.

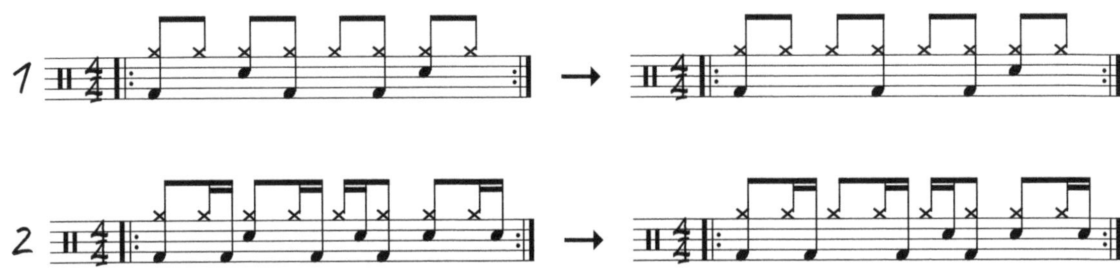

LEAVING OUT SNARE DRUM

To create more space, you can leave out the snare drum entirely.

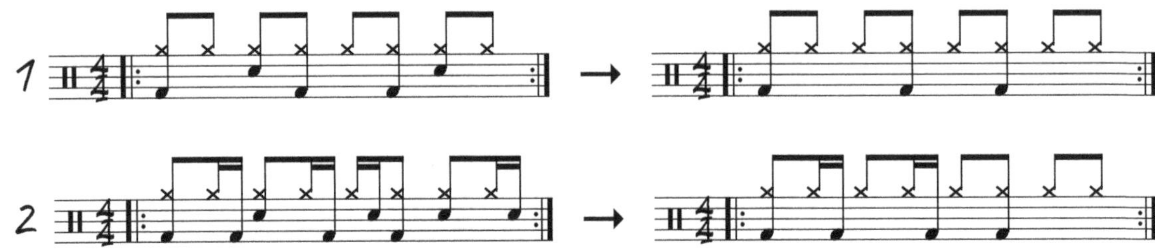

EXCHANGING KICK DRUM OR SNARE DRUM

In the examples you exchange certain notes on the snare drum with the kick drum. This can also be done the other way around.

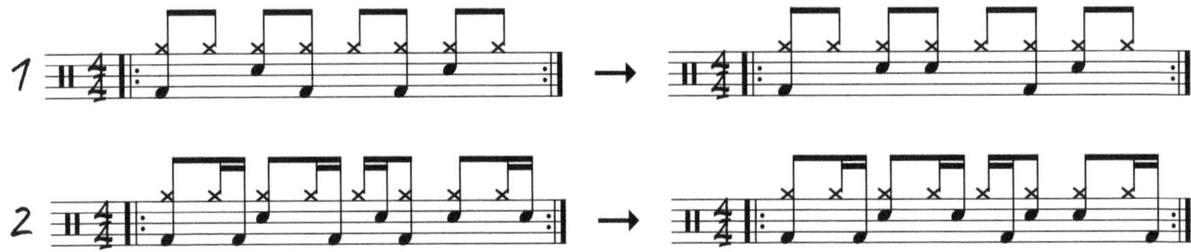

MOVING RIDING HAND

We sometimes call the right hand in a groove the "riding hand". Instead of playing the hi-hat, you play another part of the drum set with the right hand, like the ride cymbal, crash cymbal, edge of floor tom.

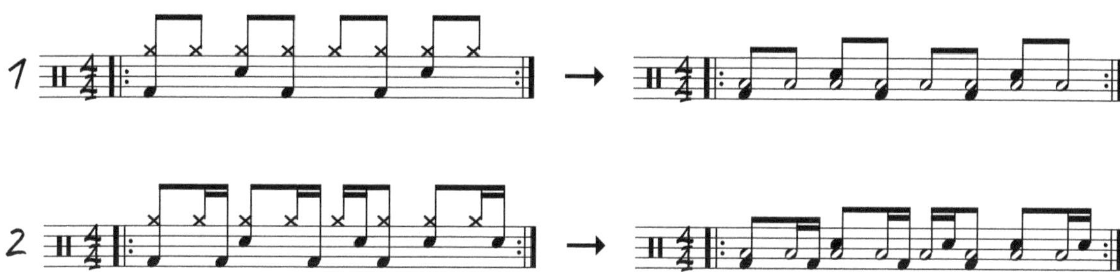

You can now play other parts with the left hand as well, like the toms or the hi-hat.

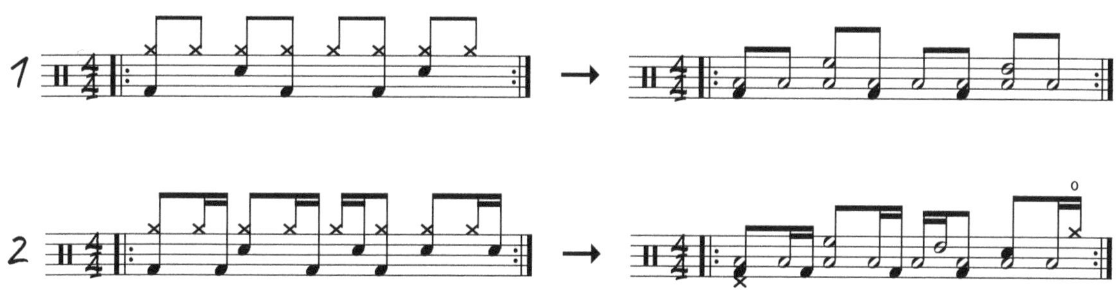

RIDELESS GROOVE

You could also leave out the "riding hand", creating a rideless groove. You now only play the groove with the snare drum and kick drum. The rhythm of the snare drum and kick drum together is the most important characteristic of the groove. You now have the possibility to play the notes on the snare drum as flams.

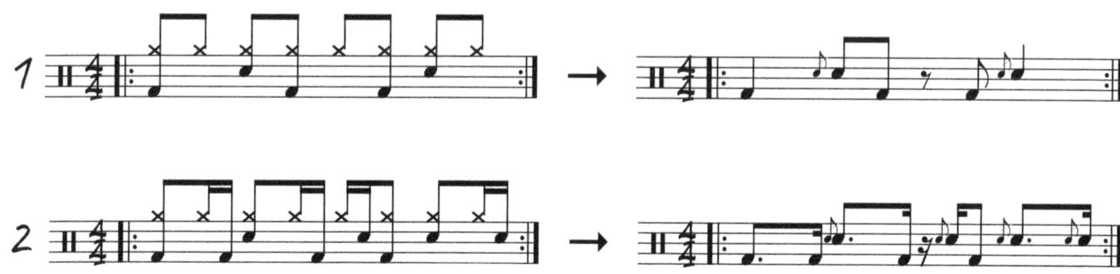

www.ingramcontent.com/pod-product-compliance
Ingram Content Group UK Ltd.
Pitfield, Milton Keynes, MK11 3LW, UK
UKHW061817190726
13853UKWH00006B/2202

9 789090 342740